D0874017

THE ROYAL PRIESTHOOD

"But ye are a chosen generation, a royal priesthood, an holy nation, a peculiar people: that ye should show forth the praises of him who hath called you out of darkness into his marvelous light."

OTHER WORKS BY THE SAME AUTHOR

RADIO TALKS
SEEKING THE OLD PATHS
THE SERMON ON THE MOUNT
THE SOUND OF THE TRUMPET
THE BIBLE VS. FALSE THEORIES
SHADOWS
HAPPY HOMES
A CLEAN CHURCH
THE KINGDOM OF THE MESSIAH
THOUGHTS ON FELLOWSHIP
COVENANTS OF GOD
THE PATH OF PEACE
THE UNITY OF THE SPIRIT
THE BROTHERHOOD OF FAITH
THE TWISTED SCRIPTURES
DEEP ROOTS
APPLES OF GOLD
GOD'S COMMUNITY
SIMPLE TRUSTING FAITH

The ROYAL PRIESTHOOD

A plea for the restoration of the priesthood of all believers in the family of God.

BY W. CARL KETCHERSIDE

MISSION MESSENGER
139 Signal Hill Drive St. Louis, Mo. 63121

THE ROYAL PRIESTHOOD

PRINTED IN UNITED STATES OF AMERICA

To Jerry and Emily
whose advice and assistance
made this volume possible.

CONTENTS

WHAT IT IS ALL ABOUT

Every child of God is a priest! Every man and woman who is a Christian has entered "the priesthood." The only high priest in God's system today is in heaven. That is the theme of this book. It is just that simple. If the Bible teaches that, this book is in harmony with the will of God; if the Bible authorizes a special priesthood composed of a clerical class, in this age, then this book is wrong in its presentation, and its author must stand condemned as one who opposes the plan of God.

I have no intent or desire to defend modern religious institutions, nor to champion the societies which have been spawned in the fertile brains of fallible men. It is my firm conviction that the community of saints planted by the holy apostles in the first generation of the Christian era constituted the divine pattern for the entire dispensation. My humble efforts will be bent, not toward the refinement, amendment, or reformation of any existing sect, but toward restoration of the primitive "colony of heaven" as representing God's ideal to which we must conform if we would meet his approval.

No careful student of the early congregation of believers can fail to be impressed with the simplicity of its worship and functioning. Imbued with a fervent zeal, motivated by a common purpose, possessed of a deep love for each other, "all the believers kept together" and "among all those who had embraced the faith there was but one heart and one soul" (Acts 2: 44; 5: 32). In such a company each felt under compulsion of spirit to do all he could to edify his fellows. None served for gain. Those who had personal property and real estate sold their possessions and distributed to all who had need; no one thought of threatening the needy with eternal destruction if they did not support a privileged class.

In the original church of God there was no distinction between clergy and laity. God's clergy (portion or lot) consisted of God's laity (people). Every member of the "laity" was a member of the "clergy" and vice versa. Every person in the divine arrangement was a minister of God. One "entered the ministry" by coming into the Christ. The holy and unblemished church can never be restored until those who love the Lord recapture in the fullest sense the picture of a "priesthood of all believers" free from the taint of a special caste.

The religious world in general has lost the pattern of the corporate worship of the original community of baptized believers. The early church gathered around a table; the modern church sits before a pulpit. The Lord placed the table in the church so it could remember its debt to him; the clergy placed the pulpit in the church to bring it in debt to them. In the early church they all spoke one by one; today all the speaking is done by one. Then the spirit was kindled; now it is quenched. Then they claimed to love each other and talked about Jesus; now they claim to love Jesus and talk about each other. In those days all exerted an effort to exhort; now all must be exhorted to exert an effort.

The primitive disciples did not ask the world to come and get the gospel, they took it to them. They gathered to eat the Lord's Supper, then scattered to preach the Word. Wherever there was a Christian and a sinner, there was a gospel meeting. They announced the glad tidings to masters and mistresses, friends and neighbors. They did it simply but fervently. They told about Jesus, his death and resurrection. They testified of their faith in him. They preached him in chariots along the road, in prison cells, by river brinks, in private homes, in halls and in synagogues. The whole earth was their auditorium, the thing at hand their pulpit.

Much of the irreverence, formality and cold ritual of these days is the result of a loss of significance of a priesthood of all believers. The sense of individual relationship to God with its attendant responsibilities has disappeared in the modern sectarian strife for supremacy of party. To restore the primitive community of saints a great reformation of thought is essential. This book has been written to help the good and honest heart properly evaluate our present status in the light of God's revelation.

PLAN OF THE BOOK

You will find the book divided into two parts. The first section is a study of the whole subject of priesthood as taught in the Bible. It deals with the reason for religion and the necessity of the priesthood in an approach unto God. It traces the history of priesthood through the Patriarchal, and Jewish dispensations, and points out the culmination of God's ideal in the Christian era which is designated as "the end of the ages."

The second division considers the arguments for a special priesthood to officiate for men "in things pertaining unto God." The case for the clergy can best be presented by that great institution which resulted from its creation, and then did the most to perpetuate and justify it. If the Roman Church cannot successfully defend the right of a special clergy to exist, no other religious organization need assume the task. That church postulates her own right to exist and to command attention of religious seekers upon the very basis of her priesthood. Destroy that foundation and the whole superstructure tumbles in disorder.

Accordingly, we chose what we believe to be the most outstanding presentation of the subject by a modern scholar. Dr. John A. O'Brien, of Notre Dame University, is universally recognized as a scholar, philosopher, and expositor. His reputation as a writer in his particular field is unexcelled. It was our good fortune, during our research, to discover in popular booklet form, his treatise entitled: *"The Priesthood—A Divine Institution."* In correspondence with the author we learned that this presentation had subsequently been incorporated as a chapter in a book which was protected by copyright. Dr. O'Brien consented to release the copyright restrictions for inclusion of the material in this book, if I would pay for the privilege of using his treatise. He suggested the sum of twenty-five dollars to be paid by me to Notre Dame. His final letter in the correspondence follows:

Dear Mr. Ketcherside:

Having received no reply to my letter of several years ago, I naturally assumed that the proposition made therein was unacceptable, and hence I am surprised by your letter.

Upon reflecting on the matter and before entering into a definite contract, I would want the assurance that various paragraphs from my writing "The Priesthood: A Divine Institution" are not to be taken out of the context in such a way as to create a misleading impression. It is with the understanding that this is not done that I am granting the requested permission in consideration of the payment of $25 to the University of Notre Dame.

The credit line to be printed should run as follows: From "The Priesthood: A Divine Institution," a chapter in *The Faith of Millions,* John A. O'Brien, Our Sunday Visitor, Huntington, Indiana, copyright 1938 by John A. O'Brien.

Looking forward to seeing a copy of your book as soon as it is published, I am,

Sincerely yours,
John A. O'Brien

The eminent theologian and Doctor of Philosophy is certainly justified in his request for proper treatment of his manuscript in any attempt at analysis and replication. For that reason we are publishing his article in its entirety, and while we are presenting it in paragraph form to make our refutation meet his argument more directly, the treatise by Dr. O'Brien will be set in distinctive type so that the interested reader by merely turning a few pages of the book between paragraphs, to the next occurrence of such type face, can read the entire article written to uphold the opinion that the special priesthood is of divine origin.

If it seems that our language is too harsh in this final section of the book, we assure you that it was not meant thus to be. The author entertains a wholesome respect for the sincere religious convictions of every man on earth, regardless of how divergent from his own views they may be. Coupled with that respect is a deep conviction of his own which makes him an implacable foe of every form of clericalism, whether exemplified in the lowliest professional preacher who serves for hire, or the pope who is looked upon as a spiritual father by millions. With such fervent feeling it is to be expected that in condemnation of a system which it is believed robs the saints of their rights and liberties, the language of exposure may sometimes be pointed, pungent and plain.

OTHER ACKNOWLEDGMENTS

The reader will observe that we have used the *Re-*

vised Standard Version of the holy scriptures more than any other version. There are numerous reasons for this, not the least of which is the personal view that this scholarly work is generally superior to most of the commonly used versions. Inasmuch as this version is copyrighted we insert herewith the authorization to use the quotations found in this book.

Dear Mr. Ketcherside:

Thank you for your letter of October 5th and your interest in the Revised Standard Version of the Bible.

This letter is your authority to use 250 selections from the Revised Standard Version through the text of your book entitled: "The Royal Priesthood." There is, of course, no fee involved, but we would ask you to state that the quotations are from the Revised Standard Version of the Bible and used by permission of the copyright owners: The National Council of the Churches of Christ in the U.S.A.

Should you require more permissions, kindly let me know.

Yours very truly,
THOMAS NELSON & SONS
W. R. McCulley
President

Credits for brief historical quotations will generally be given in conjunction with such quotations in the body of the book. It is extremely difficult after years of study to recall the many sources to which one is indebted for the formulation or crystallization of his own views, but the author desires especially to mention the following: *History of Priestcraft in All Ages and Nations,* by William Howitt (1833); *Christianity Restored* by Alexander Campbell (1835); *History of the Planting and Training of the Christian Church,* by Dr. Augustus Neander (1844); *Ministry in the Church of Christ,* by David King (1870); *The Early Church,* by David Duff, M.A., D.D., LL.D. (1891); *The Early Days of Christianity,* by Frederic W. Farrar, D.D., F.R.S. (1884); *The First Age of Christianity,* by Ernest F. Scott, D.D.,

(1926); *The Faith and Life of the Early Church,* by W. R. Slater, M.A. (1892); *Christian Worship in the Primitive Church,* by A. B. McDonald, Ph.D. (1934).

It is our sincere hope that this little volume may be a contributing factor in the stimulation of thought among those whose honest hearts make them unwilling to remain in camp halfway between Babylon and Jerusalem. This book is not exhaustive in its treatment of the subject, but suggestive in nature, and is intended to arouse God's children to think for themselves. We can never restore the primitive church until we recapture the spirit which dominated the lives of the early saints, all of whom were impelled by an unconquerable passion to know that truth which makes men free. If we can aid in any degree to a restoration of that liberty and freedom to think, speak and act, which is the divinely given heritage of every Christian, we will be satisfied.

THE DAWN OF RELIGION

In the beginning man had no religion. In the Garden of Eden he respected God, reverenced His being, and served without it. Religion belongs to sinful man. The word is formed from *re*, "back"; and *lego*, "to bind." It is that which binds man back to God. In his primeval innocence man was not separated from God, and needed nothing to bind him back. In this state the Creator freely conversed with the being made in His own image, and there was no fear in the heart of the creature, nor was there any sense of shame (Gen. 2: 22).

The advent of sin changed this happy condition. When man and his counterpart transgressed God's law, "they heard the sound of the Lord walking up and down in the garden at the breeze of the day, and the man and his wife hid themselves from the face of the Lord in the midst of the trees of the garden." When God called unto the man and asked his whereabouts, the reply was, "I heard thy voice in the garden, and I was afraid, for I was naked, and I hid myself" (Gen. 3: 8, 9). Sin produces guilt, shame and a desire for concealment. It also produced a need for religion if man is to be reconciled to God, and restored to his former condition, for iniquity makes for separation between a man and his God (Isa. 59: 2).

Inasmuch as sin is an offense against the dignity and

majesty of God, the terms of reconciliation must be dictated by the offended and not by the offender. The religion which binds man back to God must be one which originates in the divine, and not the human mind. God proposes the conditions, man must accept or reject them. Since man cannot ascertain the thoughts of God, except as He reveals them, the acceptable system of religion must be a revelation. It represents, then, not the groping, climbing, or struggling toward heaven upon a ladder erected by the trial-and-error method of human experience, but a bold approach through "a new and living way" provided by a kind and beneficent Father

GRADUAL PROCESS OF REVELATION

Every man passes through three stages of development. He is first an infant, then a child or youth, and finally attains maturity. Responsibility increases correspondingly as man's ability enables him to grasp more knowledge. What is true of each individual is also true of the body (or world) of mankind, which is composed of individuals. The social structure of humanity had its infancy, childhood and maturity. Knowledge must be gained on an ascending scale, so revelation which conveys knowledge must be bestowed on the same basis. In God's dealings with mankind, that system of religion which He endorsed, was always best adapted to man in his condition at the time, but it was also intended to fit and prepare him for reception of a fuller revelation to follow.

In fitting the world for the crowning act in which His judgment and mercy would meet, and the kingdom of heaven with its reconciling grace become a reality, God permitted the world to pass successively into three great dispensations: the Patriarchal, Jewish and Christian. Sometimes these are called, not inappropriately, the starlight, moonlight and sunlight ages, because in each succeeding one the light of truth gleamed a great deal brighter. Another age may be inserted between the second and third, and designated the twilight age. It would cover the preparatory period beginning with the announcement, by John the Immerser, of the impending kingdom, and close with the accession to the throne and coronation of our Lord. However, as the twilight is not in itself an official time of the day, but a blending of two conditions, so the world was made ready to transfer from the receding glory to the full effulgence of grace.

A word of caution needs to be inserted at this juncture. Any such designations as given above are arbitrary and serve only as matters of convenience. The great majority of mankind were not under the second, or Jewish Dispensation, at all. This pertained to the descendants of but one man, Abraham. The rest of the world remained under the Patriarchal Dispensation from its inception until the gospel was proclaimed at the house of Cornelius, by Simon Peter. It is for this reason the word "age" is not so appropriate as the word "dispensation." Since age signifies "duration" it would be impossible for two ages to run concurrently, although two dispensations may do so. Thus for 1500 years the Israelites were under the Jewish Dispensation, the while the rest of humanity continued under the Patriarchal form.

The plan of God was gradually unfolded to the world as man was able to grasp it. It was "precept upon precept, line upon line, here a little, there a little" (Isa. 28: 13). "The Kingdom of heaven is as if a man should scatter seed upon the ground, and should sleep and rise night and day, and the seed should sprout and grow, he knows not how. The earth produces of itself, first the blade, then the ear, then the full grain in the ear. But when the grain is ripe, at once he puts in the sickle, because the harvest is come" (Mark 4: 26-29). In such progressive steps man was made increasingly aware of "the eternal purpose of God" (Eph. 3: 11). But even when Christ came, he was forced to say to the apostles, "I have many things to say to you, but you cannot bear them now" (John 16: 12). Nothing is a mystery unto God, for "known unto God are all his works from the beginning of the world" (Acts 15: 18). But it was not until the Christian Dispensation that He made known "the mystery of His will, according to the purpose which He set forth in Christ, as a plan for the fulness of time" (Eph. 1: 9, 10).

SCHOOLS OF THE AGES

All instruction must be dispensed in proportion to the ability of the student to absorb it. We first send our children to the primary school, next to the elementary, and then to the high school. But each of these prepares the student for the next, and all prepare him for a better and more wholesome life. The principles gleaned in the primary school govern the child through high school and later existence. Responsibility increases as the student learns. We hold a high school student accountable for much more than one who is in the kindergarten.

In like manner God's educational process for the world involves three schools. From Adam to Moses, mankind was enrolled in the primary department, then certain chosen students were given elementary training, and now all are admissible to the high school over which Jesus is superintendent, and in which the textbook has been perfected by heaven. Our responsibility is greater now than that of the Jews who studied in the elementary school (Cp. Heb. 10: 28, 29; 12: 25).

But the principles established in former dispensations remain the same. Laws change and requirements are altered. But these are only enabling acts by which we are made more keenly aware of existing principles, and are better equipped to adapt them to our own well-being. The return to God of sinful man, the reconciliation to Him who made us and gave us being, these depend upon a disclosure of the divine will to man, an intelligent perception by man of that revelation, and humble submission unto its demands. Fortunately for those of us who now live, the things which happened in prior days, "were written down for our instruction, upon whom the end of the ages has come" (1 Cor. 10: 11). Thus, as we investigate the nature of religion which restores man to the grace of God, we cannot ignore "the first principles of God's Word" given to bring the world to the state of spiritual maturity which it should now occupy.

NATURE OF RELIGION

Just as "the sabbath was made for man, not man for the sabbath" (Mark 2: 27), so religion was made for man, and not man for religion. Religion is to cure and heal a diseased condition, and just as a remedy is not needed where there is no disease, no system for restoration to God's grace was required while man existed in the divine favor. Religion manifests itself in two departments; what God has done for us, and what God requires that we do for ourselves. The first provides proper motives to stimulate the second.

Inasmuch as sin offends God as our king, by dishonoring and insulting his majestic laws, no religion can be acceptable which does not propitiate or atone for guilt. The mere atonement for sins committed would not, however, in and of itself establish reunion, so it must have the added value of reconciliation for the offender to the offended. And since this could not be fully accomplished so long as the effect of sin, or sense of guilt remained in the conscience, there must be a feature of provision for the expiation of sin, which gives a full realization of pardon and restoration, so the sinner need not longer fear or hide himself in shame.

Sin alienates man from God. And just as a foreigner cannot dictate to a sovereign state the grounds upon which he will accept citizenship, but as the sovereign proposes the terms upon which the foreigner will be accepted for citizenship, so it is in the kingdom of heaven. Man, alienated from God, is not left to specify the terms by which he will come to God, nor are the conditions revealed by heaven the result of mere caprice or opinion. They are part of a divine system, which is the result of an eternal purpose. Man cannot dictate the laws by which he shall return to God. "There is one lawgiver and judge, He who is able to save and to destroy" (James 4: 12).

Absolute justice demands satisfaction for every sin. Sin must be expiated, or the guilty sinner must die. Expiation implies sacrifice, and this is the basis of all religion. This is true whether the religion be pagan or Christian, superstitious or rational. Sacrifice for sins constitutes a scarlet line running through God's entire revelation, from the expulsion of the first man Adam from the Edenic paradise to the death of the second man Adam upon the cross. But sacrifice demands an altar, and an altar demands a priest. Sacrifice, altar and priest—these three are the fundamental requirements of religion, and the entire word of God is given over to a revelation concerning these three items in three Dispensations. It is true that with each change of dispensation there came also a change in the priesthood (or should we state it in reverse order?) "When there is a change in the priesthood, there is necessarily a change in the law as well" (Heb. 7: 12). But changing priesthoods and changing laws did not abrogate these three essentials in either. Thus, even though we are more vitally concerned in a study of priesthood, we cannot divorce it from its basic relationship to sacrifice.

THE ELEMENT OF SACRIFICE

If no man had ever sinned, no sacrifice would ever have been offered. If no sacrifice had been required no priest would ever have served. "For every high priest is appointed to offer gifts and sacrifices" (Heb. 8: 3). "Every high priest chosen from among men is appointed to act on behalf of a man in relation to God, to offer gifts and sacrifices for sins" (Heb. 5: 1). The study of priesthood is inextricably interwoven with that of sacrifice. One cannot ignore the foundation and erect a proper structure. Yet he cannot spend so much time on the foundation as to neglect the remainder of the structure. Our consideration of the element of sacrifice in religion as revealed by our Father, will be limited to a necessary survey as a basis for further study of the priesthood of God.

The idea of sacrifice in religion is as universal as religion itself, and thus indicates the universality of the recognition of sin and the need for expiation of it. From what source did this universal idea spring, which pervaded the thought of the cultured and untutored, the civilized man and savage alike? We believe that this universal idea is a convincing proof of the common origin of all nations of mankind, and of the revelation of God to the original parent stock from which all men came. That religion is a universal part of man's existence is undenied; that sacrifice is an element in this universal concept must be admitted. What was its origin?

We have but two alternatives. It was either revealed to man or he arrived at the concept by a process of his own reasoning. This last is assumed by the learned skeptics, who are divided into two groups, those who affirm that the idea of sacrifice originated in superstition and is an invention of credulous men; and those who assert that it is an offspring of the natural sentiments of the heart.

To the believer in God neither of these can come as a satisfactory explanation. That sacrifice was not a product of man's philosophy based upon superstition is evident from the fact that God never approves as an act of worship directed unto him, that which he designates as will-worship. He instructs as follows: "See to it that no one makes a prey of you by philosophy and empty deceit, according to human tradition, according to the elemental spirits of the universe, and not according to Christ" (Col. 2: 8). He condemns as of no value those things which "have indeed an appearance of wisdom in promoting rigor of devotion and self-abasement" (Col. 2: 23). But God did approve religious sacrifices offered unto him. With reference to the first such sacrifice recorded, it is stated, "And the Lord had regard for Abel and his offering" (Gen. 4: 4). Since God never accepted as an act of devotion to himself that which originated in the superstition of men, it is obvious that the offering of sacrifice was not a product or device of superstitious ignorance.

That the idea of sacrifice did not proceed from the natural emotions and sentiments is demonstrable by the fact that no one can conceive of a connected chain of ideas by which man could arrive at the notion that slitting the throat and burning the body of an innocent animal would expiate the sin of the one who did the killing. By what inductive or deductive reasoning could man arrive at such a conclusion? Reasoning consists of the act of combining two known facts in such a manner as to produce a third and new fact, called a conclusion. What would be the established major and minor premises by which mankind universally, and in diverse circumstances, would unanimously arrive at such a conclusion? Would not primitive man, guided solely by reason, be more likely to feel that one who sinned and then slew an innocent victim only added to his guilt by such action?

The ancient Greek philosophers who soared to the heights of logic confessed their utter astonishment at the prevalence of animal sacrifice and freely admitted they could not account for it upon any rational grounds. They agreed that man could not by any chain of thinking conclude that the practice would be pleasing to the Deity. If then, the idea of killing an innocent victim could not be discovered by the light of nature or arrived at by logical thought processes, and since God would not accept what originated as mere superstition, but did accept, acknowledge and approve animal sacrifices, such sacrifices must have been by revelation of the divine mind.

The universality of sacrifice can be accounted for in the fact that all nations proceeded from the sons of Noah. "These are the families of the sons of Noah according to their genealogies, in their nations; and from these the nations spread abroad on the earth after the flood" (Gen. 10: 32). Sacrifice was taught by their common ancestor. "Then Noah built an altar to the Lord, and took of every clean animal and of every clean bird, and offered burnt offerings on the altar" (Gen.

8: 20). But Noah only followed the practice of his antediluvian fathers.

The institution of sacrifice is not mentioned by Moses in his account of man's history. Abel was the first man of whom it is recorded that he offered a blood sacrifice. However, there may be an intimation that God taught Adam and Eve to slay animals in sacrifice for we read that "the Lord God made for Adam and his wife garments of skins, and clothed them" (Gen. 3: 21). Animals were not used for food until after the flood (Gen. 9: 3), yet they were divided into clean and unclean categories before this (Gen. 7: 2). That this division was based upon use in sacrifices is shown by Genesis 8: 20. It is possible then that God showed Adam how to inflict death upon the animal victims and clothed the original pair with the skins of these animals. The Hebrew term for "atonement" is *copher* and it means "to cover." Did God cover the nakedness and shame of Adam and his wife to indicate the purpose of sacrifice or atonement?

In Hebrews 11: 4, we learn that "By faith Abel offered unto God a more acceptable sacrifice than Cain through which he received approval as righteous, God bearing witness by accepting his gifts." There are four important facts revealed here relating to Abel's sacrifice. (1) It was offered by faith, (2) It was acceptable to God, (3) Through it he received approval as righteous, (4) God accepted his gift, thus bearing witness of his approval in the divine favor. Would God accept as an act of religious exercise, approve as righteous one who performed the act, and bear witness to such righteousness by acceptance of gifts, in a matter which he had not authorized? Is it not an undeniable principle that divine authority is always essential to any acceptable worship?

Moreover, faith is the belief of testimony. Where there is no testimony there can be no faith. If Abel offered an acceptable sacrifice by faith, he must have acted upon testimony. But only the testimony of God could define what is acceptable as worship to God. "Faith comes by hearing the word of God" (Rom. 10:17). We are forced to the conclusion that the idea of sacrifice emanated from God, and was revealed to fallen man as a means of expiation for his sin, and a propitiation of God.

DEFINITION OF SACRIFICE

Alexander Campbell defined sacrifice thus: "In its literal and primary acceptance, it is the solemn and religious infliction of death upon an innocent and unoffending victim, usually by shedding its blood! Figuratively, it means the offering of anything, living or dead, person, or animal, or property to God." This definition meets our present requirements, and is therefore adopted for this volume.

Sin produces death. That which expiates sin must be that which produces life. "For the life of the flesh is in the blood; and I have given it to you upon the altar to make atonement for your souls; for it is the blood that makes atonement, *by reason of the life*" (Lev. 17: 11). For this reason, "under the law almost everything is purified with blood, and without the shedding of blood there is no forgiveness of sins" (Heb. 9: 22). But an inferior cannot atone for a superior, so "it is impossible that the blood of bulls and goats should take away sins" (Heb. 10: 4). The sacrifices of ages past were but types and shadows of the one great sacrifice, of which it is written, "But when Christ had offered for all times a single sacrifice for sins, he sat down at the right hand of God" (Heb. 10: 12).

It was by virture of this sacrifice that our Lord is frequently referred to as "the lamb of God." It was not because of his patience or humility, nor because of His life. He is called a lamb in respect to His death. His example of humility and his teaching could not expiate sin. Only by the shedding of blood could this be accomplished. When John the Immerser introduced Him it was as "the Lamb of God *who takes away the sin of the world*" (John 1: 29). In Revelation, the writer says "I saw a Lamb standing as though it had been slain" (Rev. 5: 6). In Him, priest and sacrifice met as one. "As it is, He has appeared once for all at the end of the age to put away sin by the sacrifice of himself" (Heb. 9: 26). As we study the priesthood and sacrifices of yesteryear, let us do so with but one objective, a better understanding of the priesthood and sacrifice of Him who has introduced us to "a better hope by which we draw nigh to God." The former priests were many in number, because they were prevented by death from continuing in office; but he holds his priesthood permanently, because he continues forever (Heb. 7: 23, 24).

PATRIARCHAL PRIESTS

In the revelation of God pertaining to the first age of the world, we have no lengthy theological discussions as to the nature of God, or the basis of his requirements for acceptable homage. Rather we have a rehearsal of events, of acts and facts. From these we gain our first lessons as to the character of God and His expectations of men. We learn about God by what He did. "In the beginning God created the heaven and earth." We learn about acceptable worship by observing the practice of those who engage in it. Nowhere are we given elaborate instruction concerning the introduction of sacrifice. No formal dedication, no grand presentation, marked its beginning. Had God not desired to inform us of the first murder, we would have perused the brief history of centuries without knowing that men were ministering at altars.

And we must depend for our knowledge of the priesthood of the patriarchal dispensation chiefly upon those bits of information directly connected with deeds performed. Of one thing we can be sure and that is that the principles governing intercourse with God are the same in all ages. Man must believe and obey to be acceptable with God. He may not be required to believe the same things, nor do the same things in all ages, but whatever God testifies he must believe and acting upon that faith he must obey whatever God requires of him.

The eye can only respond to the light that is available, but it must respond to that if in a healthy state. A good man in every age is the same. He is one who fulfills his obligations to God and his fellowmen as God requires of him.

Originally every man was his own priest. Incongruous though this may seem, each was his own mediator. As he stood at the altar he represented one approaching unto God in behalf of his other self—his sinful being. Such a course was essential in the infancy of the world, for as it was once right for a man to marry his own sister to establish the race, it was right for him to act as his own priest to inaugurate the spiritual system. Abel was his own priest, and so was Noah, Abraham and Isaac.

As men multiplied and families expanded, the oldest male member approached God in behalf of the others. In this simple age of time, when the world was new and men had to learn much by experience, age was the chief qualification, for it provided opportunity for greater wisdom. When children married, and lived adjacent to the father's holdings, he still sacrificed in behalf of their increasing progeny. Of such a character was the patriarch Job, for while his sons all had houses of their own, "Job would send and sanctify them, and he would rise early in the morning and offer burnt offerings according to the number of them all" (Job 1: 5). In this manner the patriarchs served in behalf of tribes or clans composed of their own descendants.

Upon the death of the father, by right of primogeniture, the firstborn son succeeded to his office as priestly mediator at the altar. It was on this basis that Esau was designated not only immoral, but *irreligious,* when he sold his birthright for a single meal (Heb. 12: 16). To despise the birthright was to despise the solemn and sacred obligation toward God, which was enjoined by it. This also enjoined upon the father a responsibility of handing on to his children the sacred traditions of God, for which cause God said of Abraham "I have chosen him, that he may charge his children and his household after him to keep the way of the Lord by doing righteousness and justice." (Gen. 18: 19). Righteousness pertains to our responsibility to God; justice to our responsibility toward our fellowmen. These two constitute the basis of all "religion that is pure and undefiled before God and the Father. . . "

Despite the dimness of the Starlight Age, it is possible to detect the pattern for future service unto God of a more elaborate nature. The occasions of the ministrations of the patriarchs in their priestly role are very informative. Let us glance briefly at some of the types of sacrifices.

(1) Thank offerings. In this category was the sacrifice of Noah when he came forth unto a world purged from sin by baptism in water. "And when the Lord smelled the pleasing odor, the Lord said in his heart, I will never again curse the ground because of man" (Gen. 8: 21).

(2) Sin offerings. That the sacrifices of Job were of this nature is evidenced by his own expression as to his reason for making the burnt offerings. "For Job said, 'It may be that my sons have sinned, and cursed God in their hearts' " (Job 1: 5).

When God became incensed at the three "friends" of Job and declared they had not told the truth about Him, he instructed them, "Now therefore take seven bulls and seven rams, and go to my servant Job, and offer up for yourselves a burnt offering; and my servant Job will pray for you, for I will accept his prayer not to deal with you according to your folly; for you have not spoken of me what is right, as my servant Job has" (Job 42: 7, 8). In this the role of expiatory sacrifice and mediatorship are clearly portrayed.

(3) Vow or dedication offerings. When Jacob was en-route to Haran, and slept all night at Luz, using a stone for a pillow, he was enabled to see a vision of God. The next morning "he took the stone which he had put under his head and set it up for a pillar and poured oil upon the top of it. . . Then Jacob made a vow" (Gen. 28:18). Years later Jacob came to the same place and set up a pillar of stone "and poured out a drink offering on it, and poured oil on it" (Gen. 35: 14). In conjunction with this incident, it is worth observing that Jacob commanded his household and all who were with him, "Put away the foreign gods that are among you, and purify yourselves, and change your garments" (Gen. 35: 2). It is quite generally agreed among scholars that the purification was by washing. Is this the forerunner of the ceremonial ablutions which were later practiced? If so, did it stem from a belief that God had cleansed the earth by water at the time of the flood? Some celebrated scholars believe this to be the case.

No study of the patriarchal sacrifices would be complete without special reference to God's confirmation of His promise to Abram. Upon the momentous occasion when it is said that Abram believed God, and it was counted unto him for righteousness, Abram asked assurance that his seed should possess the land of Canaan. God told him to bring a heifer, a goat, a ram, a turtledove and a pigeon. Abram cut the animals in two and laid each half over against the other, but he did not cut the birds in two. Through the day Abram kept the birds of prey from the carcases. After sunset, when it was dark, a smoking fire pot and flaming torch passed between the pieces, and God made a solemn covenant to give the land to the descendants of Abram, even defining the boundaries of their inheritance (Gen. 15: 7-21).

It will be noted that the animals and birds mentioned were the only ones which were later appointed for sacrifices by Abram's posterity, therefore God confirmed His covenant in the blood of every clean beast and fowl appointed for sacrifice. This very solemn method of ratification is alluded to in Jeremiah 34: 18, where the Lord declares, "And the men who transgressed my covenant and did not keep the terms of the covenant which they made before me, I will make like the calf which they cut in two and passed between its parts." The covenanting parties shed the blood of an animal, then split its body in two, placing the parts opposite to each other with a sufficient distance between that they could walk in the space, whereupon they met and joined hands in the middle of the passageway. The significance of the symbol was that each said, in effect, "May I become like this animal if I break this covenant which we have made." That is why God said, "I will make them like the calf which they cut in two."

In the case of Abram, God was the party of the first part. He was represented by the visible symbols of a smoking fire pot and a flaming torch. Abram was the party of the second part. As the patriarchal priest, representing his entire posterity, he prepared the sacrifices, and unto him God certified the covenant. By such impressive methods did God reveal his promises and wishes unto the fathers.

But the priesthood in the Patriarchal Dispensation was not limited to the descendants of Abraham, nor to the blood line of the Messiah. Every ancient nation had its chosen priests long before the tribe of Levi was selected to minister in behalf of Israel. Melchizedek, who was king of Salem, was also priest of the Most High God, among the Jebusites (Gen. 14: 18). Joseph married Asenath, daughter of the priest of On (Gen. 41: 45). Moses married Zipporah, daughter of the priest of Midian (Ex. 3: 1). The priests of Egypt were a recognized group supported from the king's treasury, for when Joseph was buying up the land of the famine-stricken inhabitants, "the land of the priests he did not buy, for the priests had a fixed allowance which Pharaoh gave them; therefore they did not sell their land" (Gen. 47: 22).

Many of the nations, even as idolatry crept in among them, retained a fear of God as a heritage from the period before the days of Peleg, in whose generation the earth was divided (Gen. 10: 25). Abraham was surprised to find a reverence for God in the heart of Abimelech, the Philistine king (Gen. 20: 11). Pharaoh said of Joseph, "Can we find such a man as this in whom is the Spirit of God?" (Gen. 41: 37). Jethro, the Midianite priest offered a burnt offering and sacrifices to God, and engaged in fellowship with Aaron and all of the elders of Israel (Exodus 18: 12). But when God separated and segregated the nation which he brought from the loins of Abraham, and committed his oracles unto them, the rest of the world without this advantage (Rom. 3: 1, 2) became dependent upon tradition and conscience.

Summarizing what we have learned about the Patriarchal Dispensation, we mention the following facts: (1) God revealed a system of religion with sacrifice, altar and priest, which was family wide in its inception; (2) Burnt offerings and sin offerings in conjunction with vows and dedication of memorable places gave hint of the type of service acceptable unto God; (3) An intimation of the need of ceremonial purification by the offerer of sacrifice is seen; (4) The selection of priestly mediators was universal among the nations; (5) The principle of atonement by blood was firmly established; (6) The death of an innocent victim for guilty sinners was clearly recognized. Such lessons aptly pointed forward to the time when the nations universally would acknowledge the need of a perfect mediator, a perfect priest and a perfect sacrifice for sins. They gave portent of an event in which the blood of an innocent being would be shed for the sins of the world. Thus did God in the Patriarchal Dispensation lay a groundwork for future revelation, and the simple lessons in the primary department of the world became a shadow of good things to come.

There remains, before we close our investigation of the priesthood in the first age of humanity, an investigation of a being of special significance, who combined within himself the offices of king and priest. We shall turn our attention briefly to this unique character in the history of religion and mankind.

PRIESTHOOD OF MELCHIZEDEK

Abram and Lot, his nephew, who had been traveling together, agreed to separate in order to avoid strife over the pasturage, so essential to their immense herds of livestock. Lot chose to dwell in the fertile plains of Jordan, and removed his family to Sodom, one of five cities in the Vale of Siddim. These cities were attacked by four kings who formed a confederacy, and who were successful in carrying off as captives, the inhabitants of the five cities, including Lot. When Abram heard of this, he pursued after the marauders, rescued their captives and retrieved the spoils. Returning from the foray, Abram passed by Salem, and thus the stage was set for meeting Melchizedek.

"And Melchizedek, king of Salem, brought out bread and wine; he was a priest of God Most High. And he blessed him and said, 'Blessed be Abram by God Most High, who has delivered your enemies into your hand!' And Abram gave him a tenth of everything" (Gen. 14: 18-20).

These three small verses of Scripture give us virtually all of the information we have in the Old Testament, relating to this patriarch. He is mentioned but once more, by David in Psalm 110: 4, where God decrees that his Son shall be made a priest forever after the order of Melchizedek. If it were not for the pointed allusions to him by the author of the New Testament book of Hebrews, we would be left to wonder at this Canaanite priest who pronounced a blessing upon the father of the Israelites, and to whom tithes were so respectfully paid.

WHO WAS MELCHIZEDEK?

A large volume could be written on the multitude of speculations concerning the identity of Melchizedek. Jewish tradition has always advanced the idea that he was Shem, who unquestionably was alive in the days of Abraham. The Targum of Jonathan says, "But Melchizedek, he is Shem, son of Noah, king of Jerusalem." With this the Jerusalem Targum agrees. There are a great many valid objections to this Jewish speculation. (1) What reason could be assigned for not calling him Shem? Moses calls him Shem in every other place. Would he be likely to make such a radical departure from his regular procedure, without proper explanation accompanying the same? (2) It is hardly probable that Shem would be reigning as king in Canaan, for Abraham was "a sojourner in a strange land," in that area. Moreover, he was told to leave his father's house, *and his kindred,* a thing he could hardly do if he came into a region over which an illustrious ancestor was a recognized monarch. (3) The apostle in Hebrews affirms that Melchizedek had no recorded father, mother or posterity. This was certainly not the case with Shem, whose lineage is easily traceable.

Another prevalent conjecture is that Melchizedek was actually the Son of God. Those who dislike to make "the father of the faithful" subservient to any tribal king of his day, advance this idea. But this would make the Son of God a type of himself, for the apostle says, "Resembling the Son of God he continues a priest forever" (Heb. 7: 3). It would hardly be logical to say that one resembled himself. Again we read, "Another priest arises in the likeness of Melchizedek." Such expressions preclude the idea that Melchizedek was the Son of God, for he would not be said to be in his own likeness, or after his own order. Moreover, the theory would make Jesus both a king and priest before His death, contrary to all Scriptural teaching on the subject.

We hold the conviction that Melchizedek was a man who was invested with both the offices of king and priest, and as such was a divinely used instrument, introduced into the sacred history of the first age that he might be re-introduced into the history of the last age, to demonstrate the superiority of an enduring priesthood over a temporary one. For this very reason, the Holy Spirit, shrouded his life in mystery, giving no clue as to his progenitors or posterity, allowing no insight into predecessors or successors. He appears on the sacred page in his full glory as monarch and mediator, he pronounces a blessing upon the father of the faithful and receives from him a tenth of the spoils he has taken. And since "it is beyond dispute that the inferior is blessed by the superior" (Heb. 7: 7) it is evident that the priest who is made after the order of Melchizedek will be superior in office and dignity to one who preceeds from the loins of Abraham.

In the primary age of the world God introduces us to a brief pre-view of a priesthood more glorious than that authorized from Sinai. Melchizedek met Abraham with bread and wine to provide physical sustenance. Our great high priest made after the same order met the children of faithful Abram with the same elements but consecrated them to a constant reminder of His sacrificial death. Abram paid tithes to Melchizedek because of his priestly relationship to God. "One might even say that Levi himself, who receives tithes, paid his ancestor when Melchizedek met him" (Heb. 7: 9, 10.). But here we must bid farewell to Melchizedek and the patriarchal dispensation in which he lived, to revert to a more thorough study of his priesthood when we have completed our investigation of that of Levi, or Aaron.

THE NATION OF ISRAEL

The Patriarchal religion was adapted to the spiritual needs of men at a time when the world was divided into families, tribes or clans. But when tribes multiplied, and came together to live a composite existence, something new was required. All of the provisions of God were made for the ultimate benefit of the whole earth. This required the coming of the Savior to offer the Supreme sacrifice once for all. However, to preserve the world until that time, it was necessary to preserve the belief in the one true God. This could be a difficult task when the whole world was creating gods of every description. It could best be achieved by the selection of one people, their separation from others, and their continued segregation. Such a people would need a definite constitution, the basic law of which would be "Thou shalt have no other gods before me," in order that they could be called back to their original purpose when they wandered from it.

Accordingly when every nation had chosen its gods, the God of heaven chose a nation. As a preparatory step He went to the land of Chaldea, and called a man whose father and grandfather were already idolaters (Josh. 24: 2). Demanding that this man separate himself from his father's house and all of his relatives, God promised to make him a great nation. Abraham "sojourned in the land of promise, as in a foreign land, living in tents with Isaac and Jacob" (Heb. 11: 9). But nomadic life is poor training for a secure national existence, for nomads want to be ever on the move. They know but little about construction of permanent cities, and resent any attempt to confine them for any length of time to a sedentary life.

Thus as a preparation for a strong national existence, the providence of God, removed the posterity of Abraham temporarily from the promised land. Making them slaves so they could not escape, He burnt out of their hearts the wanderlust which had been so much a part of their tribal existence, so that even when turned loose, they repeatedly tried to go back, choosing to endure slavery with its regular provisions of the fleshpots than a life in tents pitched in the wilderness. For several hundred years God allowed them to be confined in the most civilized nation of that day, and they were forced to learn the art of brickmaking, and labored in the construction of such storage cities as Pithom and Raamses (Exo. 1: 11). Little did the Egyptian taskmasters realize that they were schooling unwilling apprentices whose posterity would erect some of the most beautiful structures ever constructed by human hands on the hills of Zion.

When the proper time had arrived, God directed Moses to go as his ambassador to the proud and haughty court of Pharaoh. The message was, "Thus says the Lord, the God of Israel, *Let my people go!*" Moses enforced his demands with a sufficient demonstration of power that the freed captives stood upon the other side of the Red Sea. Now began the tremendous task of welding this fearful, discouraged, murmuring host of once hopeless slaves into a cohesive nation which would preserve the greatest trust ever committed to any people thus far in history.

The first essential was a constitution which would act as a rallying point. The multitude was led to the foot of a high mountain which would serve as a speaker's platform for God. Here was given one of the most startling promises ever made. First God cited what He had done for them. "You have seen what I did to the Egyptians and how I bore you on eagles' wings and brought you to myself" (Exo. 19: 4). Then He declared, "Now therefore, if you will obey my voice and keep my covenant, you shall be my own possession among all peoples, for all the earth is mine, and you shall be to me a *kingdom of priests* and a holy nation."(Exo. 19: 5, 6). This implies God's intention of making them a nation of sanctified people, each of whom might serve as a priest in his own right. Citizenship in the kingdom would constitute admission to priesthood. Observe that this was contingent upon obeying God's voice and keeping His covenant. God proposed that this people who were "His own possession" should be so holy that He could speak and commune with each of them without an earthly mediator or intervening priest.

When God's proposition was placed before the people they gave unanimous consent to it. "All that the Lord hath spoken we will do." Moses was instructed to consecrate the people for two days, so that on the third day God could address them all in a body. The people were required to wash their garments. They were to abstain from all sexual congress. Nothing that would render them unclean or act as a distracting element was to be countenanced. Bounds were placed about the mountain and the instruction was issued, "Do not go up into the mountain, or touch the border of it. Whoever touches the mountain shall be put to death; no hand shall touch him, but he shall be stoned or shot, whether beast or man, he shall not live."

On the morning of the third day there were thunders and lightnings, and a thick cloud settled upon the mountain. A loud trumpet blast caused the people to tremble. Suddenly the whole mountain quaked. The trumpet grew louder and louder. Then the voice of God came, giving the basic constitution of ten commandments. So frightened were the people that they stood afar off and shook. Then they appealed to Moses "You speak to us, and we will hear; but let not God speak to us, lest we die." Moses explained to them "God has come to test you, that the fear of Him may be before your eyes." But the people had enough. The heads of their tribes and their elders came to Moses and pleaded with him, "Go near, and hear all that the Lord our God will say; and speak to us all that the Lord our God will speak to you; and we will hear and do it" (Deut. 5: 27). They were not ready to dispense with an earthly mediator. God said to Moses, "I have heard the words of this people, which they have spoken to you, they have rightly said all that they have spoken. . . . Go, and say to them, 'Return to your tents!' But you, stand here by me, and I will tell you all the commandments and the statutes and the ordinances which you shall teach them."

While Moses was upon the mount to receive the sacred constitution the people demonstrated their unworthiness to act as a kingdom *of priests.* They gathered themselves together to Aaron, and said, "Up, make us gods, who shall go before us." At the instigation of Aaron they took off their golden ornaments, and from the precious metal he formed a calf. An altar was erected before the image, "and they rose up early on the morrow, and offered burnt offerings and brought peace offerings; and the people sat down to eat and drink, and rose up to play" (Exo. 32: 6). When Moses returned with the national constitution on two tables of stone, and saw the calf and the dancing, he threw the tables out of his hands and broke them at the foot of the mountain. He took the calf, burnt it, ground it to powder, scattered it upon the water, and made the people of Israel drink it. For once, they literally had a bellyful of idolatry!

Then Moses stood in the gate of the camp, and said "Who is on the Lord's side? Come to me." The sons of Levi gathered themselves unto him. Moses instructed them to take their swords and go through the camp slaying everyone they met. Three thousand man fell that day. (With the introduction of the law three thousand died; with the introduction of the gospel three thousand were saved. Truly the first brought death, while the second is " the law of the spirit of life in Christ Jesus.") Moses said to the tribe of Levi, "Today you have ordained yourselves for the service of the Lord, each one at the cost of his son and of his brother, that He may bestow a blessing upon you this day" (Exo. 32: 29). The holy nation and the kingdom of priests had failed in two great crises. They could not stand to hear God speak directly, when He tested them; and they had rebelled against the cornerstone of their constitution—the first and second commandments. They must have an earthly mediator and a special priesthood. The ideal of God would reach its fruition in another and a better age.

THE PRIESTHOOD OF LEVI

Prior to the formal appointment of the tribe of Levi to offer sacrifices in behalf of Israel, there were men among them recognized as priests by the congregation. When the people were gathered at Sinai to receive the law, the Lord said, "And also let the priests who come near to the Lord consecrate themselves, lest the Lord break out upon them" (Exo. 19: 22). These special priests may have been the firstborn sons of the Israelites, for they had been told previously to consecrate all of these unto the Lord (Exo. 13: 2, 15). In any event they were young men who served in this capacity, for Moses "sent young men of the people of Israel, who offered burnt offerings, and sacrificed peace offerings of oxen to the Lord" (Exo. 24: 5). They corresponded to "the young men" who were specially ordained in the church to minister in temporal matters (Acts 5: 6, 10).

In the instructions given to Moses for the construction of the tabernacle, God said, "Then bring near to you Aaron your brother, and his sons with him, from among the people of Israel, to serve me as priests—Aaron and Aaron's sons, Nadab and Abihu, Eleazar and Ithamar" (Exo. 28: 1). The priesthood being changed, there was made of necessity a change of the law (Heb. 7: 12). No longer could an Israelite offer sacrifices as in the previous dispensation. The tribe of Levi was consecrated to God in behalf of the entire congregation.

The Lord killed the firstborn of every home in Egypt to purchase redemption for Israel. For this reason he demanded in return the firstborn of every family in Israel. Then he adopted the tribe of Levi instead of the firstborn of all the tribes, thus guaranteeing the separation of the tribes until the Messiah came. God said "Behold, I have taken the Levites from among the people of Israel instead of every firstborn that opens the womb among the people of Israel. The Levites shall be mine, for all the firstborn are mine; and the day that I slew all the firstborn in the land of Egypt, I consecrated for my own all the firstborn in Israel" (Num. 3: 11-13).

Levi had three sons: Gershon, Kohath and Merari. Aaron was of the family of Kohath. Only Aaron and his direct descendants could be priests (Num. 3: 3). The rest of the descendants of Gershon, Kohath and Merari constituted the Levites. God said, "Bring the tribe of Levi near, and set them before Aaron the priest that they may minister to him. They shall perform duties for him and for the whole congregation before the tent of meeting, as they minister at the tabernacle; they shall have charge of all the furnishings of the tent of meeting, and attend to the duties for the people of Israel as they minister at the tabernacle. And you shall give the Levites to Aaron and his sons; they are wholly given to him from among the people of Israel. And you shall appoint Aaron and his sons, and they shall attend unto their priesthood; but if anyone else comes near, he shall be put to death" (Num. 3: 5, 10). All priests were Levites, but not all Levites were priests. We are especially interested in the service of the priests.

QUALIFICATIONS OF PRIESTS

1. *Genealogical.* The priest had to be a lineal des-

cendant of Aaron, and be able to establish the fact from the official records. After the Babylonian captivity there were certain claimants to the honor who "sought their registration among those enrolled in the genealogies, but they were not found there, and so they were excluded from the priesthood as unclean; the governor told them that they were not to partake of the holy food, until there should be a priest to consult Urim and Thummim" (Ezra 2: 62, 63). The Urim and Thummim were set in the breastplate of judgment which the high priest wore.

By looking into them he could determine God's judgment on any matter. The words mean "lights" and "perfections" and signified the perfect light by which the high priest could ascertain God's will in any matter of dispute.

2. *Physical.* A priest had to be physically perfect, that is, possessed of all members of the body, with each properly porportioned. One who was blind, lame, mutilated or blemished in any fashion could not minister at the altar. Such a person could be sustained by the priest's ration, but was not allowed to participate in the services (Lev. 21: 16-23). No priest was permitted to shave off the edges of his beard or to make any cuttings in his flesh (Lev. 21: 5). At the same time, the high priest was not to let the hair of his head hang loose (Lev. 21: 10).

3. *Marital.* A priest was not permitted to marry a widow, a divorcee or a prostitute. He could marry a virgin provided she was not a foreigner (Lev. 21. 7, 13, 14). It appears that a later provision permitted him to marry the widow of another priest (Ezek. 44: 22).

4. *Social.* When Nadab and Abihu, the sons of Aaron, offered unholy fire before the Lord, they were killed (Lev. 10: 1, 2). At this time God said to Aaron,

"Drink no wine nor strong drink, you nor your sons with you, when you shall go into the tent of meeting, lest you die; it shall be a statute for ever throughout your generations. You are to distinguish between the holy and the common, and between the unclean and the clean" (Lev. 10: 8-11). Were Nadab and Abihu under the influence of liquor when they took the wrong kind of fire for the incense? Such drinking was forever afterward barred to those who officiated at the sacred rites.

The high priest could not go in to any dead body nor come in contact with any corpse (Lev. 21: 10). One of the common priests could assist in the preparation and burial of the body of his father, mother, son, daughter, brother or virgin sister (Lev. 21: 1-3). Even so, he became ceremonially unclean and was not permitted to minister in any of the holy things for seven days (Ezek. 44: 26).

ORDINATION OF PRIESTS

Even though men possessed the qualifications they could not serve in the priestly office until formally ordained. Moses was told with reference to Aaron and his sons to "anoint them and ordain them and consecrate them, that they may serve me as priests" (Exo. 28: 41). The consecration ceremony is fully described in Exodus 29 and Leviticus 8. We cannot here give a detailed description. Every such ceremony should have a dual purpose. It should deeply impress the incumbents with the sacredness, dignity and seriousness of the office, and at the same time lead the people to a deep respect for a ministration authorized of God and affecting so minutely their welfare and interests. Some of the outstanding items connected with the consecration follow.

1. A sin offering was provided to enforce the need for expiation of guilt (Exo. 29: 1). Thus is illustrated the declaration that "the law appoints men in their weakness as high priests," and such men must offer sacrifices, first for their own sins and then for those of the people (Heb. 7: 27, 28).

2. The appointee was then stripped of his old garments and his whole body washed with water (Lev. 29: 4).

3. The robes of office were then placed upon him after which there was an anointing with oil. In the case of the high priest the oil was poured on so copiously that it ran down upon his beard, even "running down on the collar of his robes!" The common priests had the oil sprinkled upon them. Truly, he who was high priest was "anointed with oil above his fellows."

4. Blood was applied to the tip of the right ear, and upon the thumb of the right hand, and the great toe of the right foot of each priest. From henceforth the priest was to belong wholly to God, from head to foot. He was to hear nothing except what God wanted him to hear, do nothing God did not want him to do, and go nowhere God did not want him to walk. He was sealed with the blood of the sacrifice and as such was "God's man."

5. The period of consecration lasted for seven days. Among the Jews, the number seven indicated perfection or completeness. Thus the priests were to be wholly dedicated unto the service of God, fully consecrated before they began their ministration in behalf of others.

While Aaron and his sons were in the process of being consecrated, the altar was likewise being sanctified. "Seven days you shall make atonement for the altar and consecrate it, and the altar shall be most holy; whatever touches the altar shall become holy" (Exo. 29: 37). The word for atonement, when applied to persons means "to expiate or atone for," but with regard to things, it has the significance of "purging, cleansing, purifying." After this solemn initiation into divine service the altar not only was sanctified to God's use, but possessed the divine warrant to impart sanctity unto any offering placed upon it. To this our Lord alluded when he said to the Pharisees and scribes, "You blind men! Which is greater, the gift or the altar that makes the gift sacred?" (Matt. 23: 19).

FUNCTIONS OF LEVITICAL PRIESTHOOD

"At that time the Lord set apart the tribe of Levi to carry the ark of the covenant of the Lord, to stand before the Lord to minister to him and bless in his name, to this day" (Deut. 10: 8). This indicates a three-fold responsibility: (1) The care of the tabernacle and sacred furniture; (2) Ministration in service pertaining unto God; (3) Pronouncing the divine blessing upon the congregation. This agrees with the statement of the Lord to Aaron, "You shall attend to the duties of the sanctuary, and the duties of the altar, that there be wrath no more upon the people of Israel . . . and you and your sons with you shall attend to your priesthood for all that concerns the altar and that is within the veil, and you shall serve. I give your priesthood as a gift, and any one else who comes near shall be put to death" (Num. 18: 5, 7). To this also the New Covenant in its references to the Levitical priesthood gives assent. "Every high priest chosen from among men is appointed to act on behalf of men in relation to God, to offer gifts and sacrifices for sins" (Heb. 5: 1). "These preparations having thus been made the priests go continually into the outer tent, performing their ritual duties" (Heb. 9: 6).

RITUAL DUTIES

So multitudinous were these duties, and of such a variety, that a large volume could be filled with their enumeration and description. Time would fail us to speak of all them, so we must content ourselves with but a small number.

1. At the consecration of Aaron "fire came forth from before the Lord and consumed the burnt offering and fat upon the altar, and when all the people saw it, they shouted and fell on their faces" (Lev. 9: 24). The expression "from before the Lord" means from the Most Holy Place, where the Shekinah, or glory of God dwelt and was manifest. This fire divinely kindled was to be kept alive by refueling. "The fire on the altar shall not go out" (Lev. 6: 12, 13). It was coals of this fire which had to be used in burning incense (Lev. 16: 12), so when Nadab and Abihu "offered unholy fire before the Lord, such as he had not commanded them" (Lev. 10: 1), fire came out from before the Lord and struck them dead.

2. Each day the priests were to offer two male lambs. In this daily sacrifice one lamb was offered at the third hour of the morning, that is 9 o'clock; the other at the ninth hour of the afternoon, that is 3 o'clock (Num. 28: 3-6). It became traditional for the congregation to assemble for prayer at the time of these sacrifices (Acts 3: 1) and they abstained from eating and drinking until after the morning sacrifice was offered (Acts 2: 15). On the sabbath these sacrifices were doubled, two lambs being offered each time (Num. 28: 9, 10). The servile work necessary in presenting these sabbatical sacrifices gave occasion for our Lord's remarks as recorded in Matthew 12: 5.

The Israelites based their religious observances on

the lunar calendar. Accordingly, the priests were to offer special sacrifices to inaugurate each month. As soon as the silver trumpet sounded the appearance of the new moon, the month was officially opened with burnt offerings (Num. 28: 11-16). These are the "new moons" mentioned in Colossians 2: 16. Other regular sacrifices were made in conjunction with the three great annual festival occasions. In every case of sin, the guilty person was required to present a sacrifice before the priest, who then slew it in conformity with the ordinance.

3. The priest also acted as a judge in many instances. This was true in cases involving homicide, legal rights, or assault, where the testimony was not clear. The Israelites were instructed that, "in any case within your towns which is too difficult for you, arise and go up to the place which the Lord your God will choose, coming to the Levitical priests and the judge who is in office in those days, you shall consult them, and they shall declare to you the decision" (Deut. 17: 8, 9). Such a decision was final and could not be altered. "You shall be careful to do according to all that they direct you; according to the instructions which they give you, and according to the decision which they pronounce to you, you shall not turn aside from the verdict which they declare to you, either to the right hand or to the left" (Deut. 17: 10, 11).

False accusers were to receive summary discipline. "If a malicious witness arises against any man to accuse him of wrongdoing, then both parties shall appear before the Lord, before the priests and the judges who are in office in those days; the judges shall enquire diligently, and if the witness is a false witness, and has accused his brother falsely, then you shall do to him as he had meant to do to his brother; so you shall purge the evil from the midst of you."

One of the most interesting and peculiar decisions in which the priest assisted pertained to a woman whose husband suspected she was guilty of carnal relationship with another man. The priest took holy water in an earthen vessel, and mixed it with dust scraped off the tabernacle floor. The woman was forced to drink the water, and if she was guilty of unconfessed crime, the water caused intense abdominal pain which was accompanied by bodily swelling and other symptoms. An innocent woman suffered no such ill effects. The record declares, "This is the law in cases of jealousy" (Num. 5: 29).

The priest was to determine when a man had contracted leprosy. Anyone who had an indication of the disease was to be examined and isolation was the fate of those afflicted. When one was pronounced unclean by the priest, he was compelled to wear torn clothing, let the hair of his head hang loose, cover his upper lip, and cry, "Unclean, unclean" when anyone approached. He was banished from his home and forced to dwell outside the camp (Lev. 13: 45). Often such unfortunates dwelled in tombs as the only available shelters. If the disease ran its course and the leper believed himself to be free from its ravages he could present himself to the priest who made a thorough investigation. If the man proved to be free of the disease he performed a ritual for ceremonial cleansing and return to society (Lev. 14). It was because of this requirement that Jesus commanded the leper whom he had physically cleansed, "Go and show yourself to the priest, and make an offering for your cleansing as Moses commanded for a proof to the people" (Luke 5: 14).

4. Aaron and his sons were to superintend the taber-

nacle. When the signal was given to march they dismantled the tabernacle, covered all of the articles of furniture, and prepared them for transportation. Then the Kohathites came near and the priests assigned to each man his task and his burden. They did the same for the Gershonites and Merarites who were charged with the actual transportation of all the essential equipment from place to place. Later, when the temple was built, the priests lived round about it as guards. They also opened the building every morning (1 Chron. 9: 27). The utensils of service had to be carefully checked in and out, the spices had to be mixed for the incense, and the shewbread baked every sabbath (1 Chr. 9: 28-32). These tasks fell to the priests.

DAY OF ATONEMENT

Special mention needs to be made of this great day, which was observed annually on the tenth day of the seventh month. This month was ushered in with a festival of trumpets. The first day was to be observed as a day of solemn rest, a memorial day (Lev. 23: 23-25). This is the great Jewish New Year still observed by Jews throughout the world.

Beginning at sunset on the ninth day of this month, the day of national expiation was ushered in to be observed until the close of the following day. It was the only day of fasting specifically commanded the Jews by the Old Testament, and during this entire day they were to partake of no refreshment, but rather "afflict their souls" (Lev. 23: 27). Luke refers to it in Acts 27: 9. Upon this fateful day the high priest entered the holy of holies. No common priest was ever permitted to enter this sacred apartment, and even the high priest was restricted to this occasion as a representative of the nation (Lev. 16:2). He was required to select a young bullock for a sin offering and a ram for a burnt offering. Divesting himself of his rich robes of office, he donned white linen clothing, for on this day he stood upon an equality with others, being forced to offer for his own sins as well as for those of the people.

He then took two goats for a sin offering for the people, and after presenting them before the Lord, he placed two pieces of gold in a small box. On one appeared the words "For the Lord," and on the other "For Azazel" which is translated "scapegoat" in the King James Version. The pieces of gold were drawn out and placed upon the heads of the goats. The one upon which the Lord's lot fell was destined to be slain.

The high priest killed the bullock for his own sins and caught the blood. He then filled the golden censer with coals of fire from the altar and put incense upon them. This incense created a fragrant smoke which veiled the mercy seat. Then the high priest sprinkled the blood with his finger before the mercy seat seven times. Then coming out, he killed the goat for the sins of the people, and took its blood into the most holy place and sprinkled it upon and before the mercy seat.

Afterwards the goat which remained alive was brought, and the high priest confessed over it all the iniquity and transgressions of Israel, putting them upon the head of the goat which was then sent away into the wilderness by a man in readiness (Lev. 16: 21). It is said, "The goat shall bear all their iniquities upon him to a solitary land." (Lev. 16: 22). Then the high priest went into the tent of meeting, took off his linen garments, bathed his body in water, and put on his ministering garb and continued the ritual activities demanded. The writer of Hebrews makes numerous references to this day of atonement, of which he says, "Into the second only the high priest goes, and he but once a year, and not without taking blood which he offers for himself and for the errors of the people. By this the Holy Spirit indicates that the way into the sanctuary is not yet opened as long as the outer tent is still standing (which is symbolic for the present age)" (Heb. 9: 7-9).

A COPY AND SHADOW

We must not forget our original premise that in each dispensation, God prepared mankind for the reception of greater revelations in succeeding dispensations. We live in the final age of the earth. The apostle declares that those things which happened to God's ancient people "were written down for our instruction, upon whom the end of the ages has come" (1 Cor. 10: 11). Again he states, "For whatever was written in former days was written for our instruction, that by steadfastness and by the encouragement of the scriptures we might have hope" (Rom. 15: 4). We should be deeply grateful as we read of the priesthood of the past ages that "God had foreseen something better for us" (Heb. 11: 40).

It is a proof of the divinity of the Bible that it contains a shadow or likeness of a substance or body which did not yet exist. To have a shadow, three things are required: a substance, a light, and a reflection. We cannot create a shadow from a non-existent substance. Only God could create a shadow first, then bring into existence the substance, so that the light of truth directed against it would reveal the exactness of the shadow. The service of the Old Covenant priesthood constituted a type of our service and sanctuary in the Christian era. "They serve as a copy and shadow of the heavenly sanctuary, for when Moses was about to erect the tent, he was instructed by God, saying 'See that you make everything according to the pattern which was shown you on the mountain' " (Heb. 8: 5). "For Christ has entered not into a sanctuary made with hands, a copy of the true one, but into heaven itself" (Heb. 9: 24). "These are only a shadow of what is to come; but the substance belongs to Christ" (Col. 2: 17). As the substance is superior to a shadow, so is the present system superior to that which preceded it.

But since a reflection bears a resemblance to that which it shadows, so may we learn of God's plan and purpose by studying the former priesthood. The record thereof is a part of those former things written for our instruction. We propose a few suggestions along this line to encourage the student into greater research in God's former revelation.

THE HIGH PRIEST IN TYPE

The high priest of the Old Covenant foreshadowed Christ. Both were specially called of God to their positions. "One does not take the honor upon himself, but he is called by God, just as Aaron was. So also Christ did not exalt himself to be made a high priest, but was appointed by him who said to him, 'Thou art my Son, today have I begotten thee.' " (Heb. 5: 4, 5). There could be but one high priest at a time under the Levitical regime, there can be but one high priest any time during this dispensation. "He holds his priesthood permanently, because he continues forever" (Heb. 7: 24).

Both Aaron and Christ were ordained to serve in behalf of others in matters pertaining unto God. Aaron was vested with special robes of office, created for glory and beauty. Isaiah pictures our Lord as "glorious in his appeal, marching in the greatness of his strength" (Isa. 63: 1). When the seer upon Patmos beheld him, he was clothed with a long robe and with a golden girdle about his breast (Rev. 1: 13). The ancient high priest had written across his mitered brow "Holiness to the Lord." When the conquering Christ appeared to John, he portrayed him thus, "On his head are many diadems; and he has a name inscribed which no one knows but himself. He is clad in a robe dipped in blood and the name by which he is called is The Word of God . . . On his robe and on his thigh he has a name inscribed, King of kings and Lord of lords" (Rev. 19: 12, 13, 16).

When the high priest served in his mediatorial robe, he bore upon his breast and next to his heart the names of all of the tribes in whose behalf he officiated. Their names were upon the onyx stones on his shoulders and in the precious stones upon his bosom. Just as he could never forget those whose care weighed heavily upon him, and for whom he interceded before the mercy seat, so our high priest carries a sympathetic understanding of all our needs. "For we have not a high priest who is unable to sympathize with our weaknesses, but one who in every respect has been tempted as we are, yet without sinning. Let us then with confidence draw near to the throne of grace, that we may receive mercy and find grace to help in time of need" (Heb. 4: 15, 16.).

Aaron began his public ministry by being washed, the act being performed by Moses. Our Lord began his personal ministry by being washed in the waters of baptism, the immersion being performed by John the Immerser. Aaron was anointed with oil which was poured upon him so generously that it ran down upon his beard and the collar of his coat. The lesser priests were anointed with the same oil but not in such a measure. Even so our Lord was anointed with the Spirit sent down from heaven. It was this anointing which "Christed" him, and it was not given to him by measure (John 3: 34).

In his official capacity Aaron was a mediator, standing between God and the people. Now "there is one God, and there is one mediator between God and men, the man Christ Jesus" (1 Tim. 2: 5). Aaron was also a judge, and by the aid of the Urim and Thummim, he could render a perfect decision from which no appeal could be made. The apostle declares that God "has fixed a day on which he will judge the world in righteousness by a man whom he has appointed, and of this he has given assurance to all men by raising him from the dead" (Acts 17: 31). Jesus said, "The Father judges no one, but has given all judgment to the Son" (John 5: 22).

The high priest secured atonement for all of the nation. It was he who took the blood into the holiest of all, and there behind the veil, sprinkled it before the mercy seat. This had to be repeated annually. "But when Christ appeared as a high priest of the good things that have come, then through the greater and more perfect tent, he entered once for all into the Holy Place, taking not the blood of goats and calves but his own blood, thus securing eternal redemption" (Heb. 9: 11, 12). "Nor was it to offer himself repeatedly, as the high priest enters the Holy Place yearly with blood not his own; for then he would have had to suffer repeatedly since the foundation of the world. But as it is, he has appeared once for all at the end of the age to put away sin by the sacrifice of himself."

It is observable that on the day of atonement the high priest was forced to carry out the ritual alone. "There shall be no man in the tent of meeting when he enters to make atonement in the holy place" (Lev.

16: 17). Our high priest also was bereft of all help in his great sacrificial atonement for the world. There was no friend to aid. His response as made by the prophet was, "I have trodden the wine press alone, and from the peoples no one was with me" (Isa. 63: 3).

We must not forget that it is impossible for that which is weak and finite to perfectly portray that which is perfect. Consequently there must be discrepancies in the comparison of the priesthoods, and points of contrast as well as of similarity. Some of these are mentioned by the sacred writers. The ancient high priests became such by fleshly descent, but of Christ it is stated, "Who has become a priest, not according to a legal requirement concerning bodily descent but by the power of an indestructible life" (Heb. 7: 16). Again, those who formerly became priests took their office without an oath, but this one was addressed with an oath, "The Lord has sworn, and will not change his mind, Thou art a priest forever" (Heb. 7: 21). Then, too, the former priests were many in number, because they were prevented by death from continuing in office; but he holds his priesthood permanently, "because he continues forever" (Heb. 7: 23, 24).

THE COMMON PRIESTS

The priests associated with Aaron were typical of all Christians, associated with our great high priest in the service of God. Every Christian is consecrated and sanctified as a priest, there are many priests. Besides these there are no other priestly orders recognized by heaven. There can be no hierarchical distinctions in the church. Every priest of God is of equal dignity in the divine arrangement. There is no distinction between a clergy and laity.

The common priests of the Old Covenant were all

sons of high priests. Their priesthood grew out of their relation to him. They became priests because they were born into his family. Thus it is in this dispensation. We are priests of God because of our relationship to Christ and for no other reason. We become priests by being born again. Those steps which are required to make us sons and daughters of the Lord Almighty, introduce us into the priesthood. There was no priesthood for Aaron's descendants separate and apart from his priesthood, there is none for us out of Christ. It is only as he lives in us and we live in him that we become a kingdom of priests unto God.

In many respects the consecration of Aaron and his sons was alike. They were made partakers of the same ritual for sanctification in their priestly functions. In like manner our Lord "though he was in the form of God, did not count equality with God a thing to be grasped, but emptied himself, taking the form of a servant, being born in the likeness of men." (Phil. 2: 6, 7). "For he who sanctifies and those who are sanctified have all one origin. That is why he is not ashamed to call them brethren" (Heb. 2: 10). Accordingly, some of those features required to begin the personal ministry of our Lord are requisite to introduce us to our ministration as priests. We, too, must be washed in the waters of baptism, and the gift of the Spirit is made to us upon completion of this initiatory rite (Acts 2: 38; 5: 32). Certainly we do not receive the measure of the Spirit as poured out upon Christ, but we are anointed with the Spirit as sons of God (Gal. 4: 6).

The ancient priests required first a blood sacrifice before they could be consecrated. The same holds true for ourselves. They were required to put off their old garments; we are required to "hate the garment spotted by the flesh" (Jude 23). They were required to be completely washed in the laver; we must submit to "the washing of regeneration" (Titus 3: 5). They were adorned with robes of glory and beauty; we are to "Put on then, as God's chosen ones, holy and beloved, compassion, kindness, lowliness, meekness and patience" (Col. 3: 12). They received an application of the anointing oil when washed; we are saved "by the washing of regeneration and renewal in the Holy Spirit, which he poured out upon us richly through Jesus Christ our Savior" (Titus 3: 5, 6).

The priests of the former dispensation were made such by obedience to the commands of God. Moses could not originate, devise or invent ceremonies, rituals, or modes of induction. At the very outset "Moses said to the congregation, 'This is the thing which the Lord has commanded to be done' " (Lev. 8: 5). Nothing else would have been accepted or recognized by heaven. Those who were introduced by some other form would never have been accepted or recognized as priests. In like manner, those who today have not been baptized into Christ can never be accepted as priests of God. Only God can stipulate those terms by which men may approach unto him in acceptable service. No substitutionary measures will be allowed to stand.

The Old Covenant priests were ordained to serve and not to be served. They were set apart to minister and not to be ministered unto. Every priest of God, sanctified to his service, was expected to engage actively in that service. The priests did not hire a substitute to officiate in their places. Priesthood conferred a special personal obligation to minister unto God and to others. This obligation grew out of relationship to the sanctuary and to God. True, the priests did not all do the same thing at the same time, but they did in turn whatever service was required and whatever fell their lot at any given time. It is said of Zechariah "Now while he was serving as priest before God when his division was on duty, according to the custom of the priesthood, it fell to him by lot to enter the temple of the Lord and burn incense" (Luke 1: 8, 9). Is there not a lesson in this for God's priests today to qualify themselves to do anything required in the service of God, when it may fall their lot to do it? Aaron and his sons were ordained to "serve God as priests" (Exo. 28: 1), and not to be served. Unless God's people today personally minister unto him as priests they void his plan, and defeat his eternal purpose.

The blood of the sacrifice was applied to the extremities of each priest. It was placed upon the tip of his right ear, on the thumb of the right hand, and on the great toe of the right foot. This dedicated the whole body to God. From this time forward he was "God's man." It was not enough that the sacrifice be killed and the blood shed. That blood had to be applied to each individual. Thus it is also with God's priests. The blood must be applied to each heart. "For if the sprinkling of defiled persons with the blood of goats and bulls and with the ashes of a heifer sanctifies for the purification of the flesh, how much more shall the blood of Christ, who through the eternal Spirit offered himself without blemish to God, purify your conscience from dead works to serve the living God" (Heb. 9: 13, 14). It is in view of this that the record declares, "Therefore, brethren, since we have confidence to enter the sanctuary by the blood of Jesus . . . let us draw near with a true heart in full assurance of faith, with our hearts sprinkled clean from an evil conscience and our bodies washed with pure water" (Heb. 10: 19, 22). The Christian is God's man. He belongs wholly unto God. "You are not your own; you were bought with a price. So glorify God in your body." (1 Cor. 6: 19, 20). A Levitical priest met death if he forgot the sanctification of the blood. "How much worse punishment do you think will be deserved by the man who has spurned the Son of God, and profaned the blood of the covenant by which he was sanctified, and outraged the Spirit of grace?" (Heb. 10: 29.)

The most holy place was a type of heaven. Into it only the high priest went, "and he but once a year, and not without taking blood which he offers for himself and for the errors of the people. By this the Holy Spirit indicates that the way into the sanctuary is not yet opened as long as the outer tent is still standing" (Heb. 9: 7, 8). The holy place before the curtain represents the church. It was here the common priests ministered. "The priests go continually into the outer tent, performing their ritual duties" (Heb. 9: 6).

In the outer tent stood the table containing the bread of the Presence. There were twelve loaves, one for each tribe. This bread could be eaten only by the priests, and had to be eaten in the tent. It was changed once every seven days, and was eaten at that time. The Lord has a table in his church today. It contains the bread of His Presence. There is but one loaf upon it, because there is no longer any tribal distinction. "Thou wast slain and by thy blood didst ransom men from every tribe and tongue and people and nation, and hast made them a kingdom and priests to our God, and they shall reign on earth" (Rev. 5: 9, 10). "Because there is one loaf, we who are many are one body, for we all partake of the same loaf" (1 Cor. 10: 17). The hallowed bread can only be eaten by God's priests, by Christians. It is wrong to offer it to those who have not been sanctified by obedience to the commands of God. It is to be eaten by God's priests once every seven days. In the primitive church the disciples met together upon the first day of the week to break bread.

The only source of light in the tabernacle was the golden lampstand. It consisted of a center shaft which supported three branches or divisions on either side. These received their strength from their attachment to the center shaft. In all there were seven lamps, the number seven signifying perfection to the Jews. There is but one source of light in the church, the Word of God. It is a perfect light. The testimony concerning Christ as given by Matthew, Mark, Luke, and John constitutes the center support. The three divisions of God's revelation previously given all point forward to Christ. Christ said, "These are my words which I spoke to you, while I was still with you, that everything written about me in *the law* of Moses and *the prophets* and the *Psalms* must be fulfilled" (Luke 24: 44). The three divisions following: history, epistolary and prophecy (Acts, epistles and Revelation) all point backward to Christ. Destroy the center shaft and all would fall. It was the duty of the priests in the Mosaic dispensation to attend to the lamps daily. They were to see that these lamps were always prepared to shine brightly, and that they were "set up so as to give light upon the space in front of it" (Lev. 25: 37). The priests of God now should daily attend unto the study and proclamation of God's Word. This was true in the primitive church. "Every day in the temple and at home they did not cease teaching and preaching Jesus as the Christ" (Acts 5: 42).

The golden altar also stood in the holy place. Upon it incense was burnt to send up a sweet odor before the mercy seat of God. The incense was burnt every morning and every evening (Exo. 30: 7, 8). In Revelation 5: 8 we read of "golden bowls full of incense, which are the prayers of the saints." The psalmist entreated, "Let my prayer be counted as incense before thee, and the lifting up of my hands as an evening sacrifice" (Psalm 141: 2). Surely God's priests in this age should minister daily at "the golden altar"; for we are instructed, "Through him then let us continually offer up a sacrifice of praise to God, that is, the fruit of lips that acknowledge his name" (Heb. 13: 15).

It is with reluctance we conclude this chapter. We are fully aware that we have not plumbed the depths of God's great typical institution, and shall be content if, having scratched the surface, we may encourage the reader to dig ever deeper, and like the husbandman of the parable "of his treasure bring forth things new and old." We stand lost in wonder and amazement at the spiritual negative from which the perfected picture has been developed, expecially when we contemplate that the negative was made before the body existed to be photographed. When the body was at last brought into existence, the negative was shown to be a perfect reproduction. "Known unto God are all his works from the beginning."

A PROFANE PRIESTHOOD

"Her prophets are wanton, faithless men; her priests profane what is sacred, they do violence to the law" (Zeph. 3: 4). The writer of the Hebrew letter asserts that the high priest under the Mosiac law could "deal gently with the ignorant and wayward, since he himself is beset with weakness" (Heb. 5: 2). Speaking of our Lord, it is affirmed, "He has no need, like those high priests, to offer sacrifices daily, first for his own sins and then for those of the people" (Heb. 7: 27).

The human weakness of the priests was early manifested in their career. Perhaps the first defection in their religious ministration came about when Nadab and Abihu "each took his censer, and put fire in it, and laid incense on it, and offered unholy fire before the Lord, such as he had not commanded them" (Lev. 10: 1). Their sin was that of substitution of something else for what God had specified as essential in worship. As a result they were divinely disciplined, and fire came from the most holy place to devour them. The intimation is that they were under the influence of intoxicants and thus in a confused mental state in which they could not distinguish "between the holy and the common, and between the unclean and the clean." In any event, the sin was as inexcusable then as it is now. The punishment of their dereliction was so startling that it had a sobering effect upon the remaining priests.

However, as generations drifted by, the priests fell victim to their own lusts, and exercised an evil influence upon the congregation.

When Eli was priest, his sons "were worthless men, they had no regard for the Lord" (1 Sam. 2: 12). They were covetous and greedy. A custom had been introduced that when a man offered a sacrifice, the servant of the priest would come with a three-pronged fork in his hand which he would thrust into the kettle or pot of boiling meat. All that the fork brought up the priest appropriated for his own consumption. Too, the priest's servant demanded of those who sacrificed a choice piece of raw meat for roasting with the fat still attached. Inasmuch as the law demanded that all of the fat be burnt, and none be eaten, the offerer might protest, saying, "Let them burn the fat first and then take as much as you wish," whereupon the reply would be made, "No, you must give it now; and if not, I will take it by force." As a result, "the sin of the young men was very great in the sight of the Lord; for the men treated the offering of the Lord with contempt" (1 Sam. 2: 12-17).

Added to these faults were grave immoralities, for the priests engaged in illicit intercourse, with the women who served at the entrance to the tent of meeting. So flagrantly notorious was this crime, that Eli said, "Why do you do such things? For I hear of your evil doings from all the people. No, my sons; it is no good report that I hear the people of the Lord spreading abroad." However, they paid no attention to the remonstrance of their father, and a prophet was sent to Eli with the fateful news of the loss of the priesthood to his posterity.

The words of the man of God were very significant. "Why then look with greedy eye at my sacrifices and my offerings which I commanded, and honor your sons above me by fattening yourself upon the choicest parts of every offering of my people Israel. . . Behold the days are coming when I will cut off your strength and the strength of your father's house, so that there will not be an old man in your house. Then in distress you will look with envious eyes on all the prosperity which shall be bestowed upon Israel; and there shall not be an old man in your house for ever. The man of you whom I shall not cut off from my altar shall be spared to weep out his eyes and grieve his heart; and all the increase of your house shall die by the sword of men. . . . And I will raise up for myself a faithful priest who shall do according to what is in my heart and in my mind; and I will build him a sure house, and he shall go in and out before my anointed for ever. And every one who is left in your house shall come to implore him for a piece of silver, and a loaf of bread, and shall say, 'Put me, I pray you, in one of the priest's places, that I may eat a morsel of bread" (1 Sam. 2: 29-36).

In view of the above, George Bush, Professor of Hebrew and Oriental Literature, New York City University, says in his *Notes on Leviticus*: "Aaron was succeeded by Eleazar, his eldest surviving son, after the death of Nadab and Abihu, and it continued in his family through seven generations, till the time of Eli. On his death it was removed from the branch for the wickedness of Eli's sons and given to the descendants of Ithamar, Aaron's other son. In the time of Solomon it returned again into the line of Eleazar, in which it continued until the Babylonish captivity. Jeshua, the first high priest after the return of the Jews, was of the same family, but after his time the appointment became very uncertain and irregular; and after Judea became a Roman province, no regard whatever was paid to this part of the original divine institution. The office was in fact in process of time so far desecrated in the general corruption, that it was often sold to the hightest bidder, whether of the family or not; and so things continued, till finally the nation had filled up the measure of its iniquities, and priest, altar and temple were all swept away in the abolition of the Jewish economy and the dispersion of the race." (pp. 73, 74).

The decadence of the priesthood is easily traceable in the sacred scriptures, and this condition is assigned as one of the basic reasons for the grievous transgressions which resulted in the exile of the people to Babylon. As early as chapter 17 of Judges we read of a young man of the tribe of Levi contracting to be a priest for a family at a stipulated salary of ten pieces of silver, a suit of clothing and his living on an annual basis. "And Micah installed the Levite, and the young man became his priest, and was in the house of Micah. Then Micah said, 'Now I know that the Lord will prosper me, because I have a Levite for a priest'" (Judges 17: 12, 13). The fact that he expected to officiate before both a graven and molten image did not seem to trouble the mercenary Levite. Later when a group of marauders from the tribe of Dan were stealing the household gods the "priest" enquired as to their intentions. "And they said to him, 'Keep quiet and put your hand upon your mouth, and come with us, and be to us a father and a priest. Is it better for you to be priest to the house of one man, or to be priest to a tribe?' And the priest's heart was glad; he took the ephod, and the teraphim, and the graven image, and went in the midst of the people" (Judges 18: 18-20). He had received a call to pastor a larger church!

By the time of Isaiah, stern indictments were hurled against the profligates. "The priest and prophet reel with strong drink; they err in vision, they stumble in giving judgment" (Isa. 28: 7). Jeremiah declared, "An appalling and horrible thing has happened to the land: the prophets prophesy falsely, and the priests rule at their direction; my people love to have it so, but what will you do when then end comes?" (Jer. 6: 31). With the prophets erring in their vision, and presenting false messages, and the priests by their direction stumbling in giving judgment, conditions became ever more serious for God's people. The condition was augmented by virtue of the fact that the people preferred smooth prophecies to the real truth. They were willing to support men who taught error and reassured them that God's vengeance would not come, but they starved the occasional faithful bearer of heaven's real message. "For from the least to the greatest of them, every one is greedy for unjust gain; and from prophet to priest, every one deals falsely. They have healed the wound of my people slightly saying 'Peace, peace,' when there is no peace" (Jer. 6: 13, 14). So brazen had they become that the word says they were not only unashamed, but actually did not know how to blush.

Their religious leaders acted in collusion to maintain their mercenary positions. "Both prophet and priest are ungodly, even in my house have I found their wickedness, says the Lord. Therefore their way shall be to them like slippery paths in the darkness, into which they shall be driven and fall; for I will bring evil upon them in the year of their punishment, says the Lord" (Jer. 23: 11, 12). The faithful Jeremiah warned, "Do not listen to the words of the prophets who prophesy to you, filling you with vain hopes; they speak visions of their own minds, not from the mouth of the Lord. They say continually to those who despise the word of the Lord, 'It shall be well with you,' and to everyone who stubbornly follows his own heart, they say, 'No evil shall come upon you.'" Apparently the religious teachers were willing to provide whatever the people were anxious to hear, if they were well paid for it. It was a case of "like people, like priest" (Hosea 4: 9).

Almost without exception the men of God who were sent to declare the burden of God's people, included the priests in their condemnatory pronouncements. Micah said, "Its priests teach for hire, its prophets divine for money; yet they lean upon the Lord and say, 'Is not the Lord in the midst of us? No evil shall come upon us.'" (3: 11). It needs to be remarked that God had provided for the sustenance of his priests. They were entitled to a portion of the offerings made upon the altar. "Do you not know that those who are employed in the temple service get their food from the temple, and those who serve the altar share in the sacrificial offerings?" (1 Cor. 9: 13). The condemnation by Micah was not because the priests were financially supported in teaching, but because they had professionalized the God-given task and were doing so because of the money they got for it. No longer satisfied to trust in God and their brethren to supply them with voluntary gifts at the altar, they were now hiring themselves out for wages and teaching for gain. It is not injurious to say that the apostle declares in the verse following the one where he reasons that the priests get their food from the temple, "In the same way, the Lord commanded that those who proclaim the gospel should get their living by the gospel" (1 Cor. 9: 14). Will God be as certain to condemn those who today "teach for hire?"

Zephaniah referred to Jerusalem as a rebellious, defiled and oppressing city. He declared that she listened to no voice, accepted no correction, and refused to draw near to God. The reason may be found in his assertion that "Her officials within her are roaring lions; her judges are evening wolves that leave nothing until the morning. Her prophets are wanton, faithless men; her priests profane what is sacred, they do violence to the law" (Zeph. 3: 3, 4). Malachi is especially stern. He accused the priests of lacking both respect and reverence. "A son honors his father, and a servant his master, 'If then I am a father, where is my honor? And if I am a master, where is my fear?' says the Lord of hosts to you, O priests, who despise my name" (Mal. 1: 6).

God declares that his covenant with Levi was one of life and peace, given to him that he might fear. He affirms that "He feared me, he stood in awe of my name. True instruction was in his mouth, and no wrong was found on his lips. He walked with me in peace and uprightness, and he turned many from iniquity. For the lips of a priest should guard knowledge, and men should seek instruction from his mouth, for he is the messenger of the Lord of hosts." That the priestly function had been prostituted from its original purpose is evident as the man of God continues, "But you have turned aside from the way; you have caused many to stumble by your instruction; you have corrupted the covenant of Levi, says the Lord of hosts, and so I make you despised and abased before all the people, inasmuch as you have not kept my ways but have shown partiality in your instruction" (Mal. 2: 5-9).

As a result of the corruption and idolatry which engulfed the inhabitants of Jerusalem they were carried into Babylon. Here, in a state of desperation, God burnt out of their hearts a love for other gods. At the end of seventy years they were released to return to

Jerusalem where they labored arduously to restore the city and its walls. Among them were many priests and Levites as well as temple servants. The desire to follow the word of God is manifested in the fact, that when certain ones of the priests sought their registration among the genealogies, and could not locate their names, they were excluded from the priesthood as unclean. "The governor told them that they were not to partake of the most holy food, until a priest with Urim and Thummim should arise" (Neh. 7: 65).

However, as generations passed on, the lessons were forgotten, and by the time our Lord was born the priesthood had become the pawn of crafty politicians. When Judea became a Roman protectorate, there was often a conflict between the Jews and their conquerors, so that sometimes two high priests were recognized at the same time. An indication of the unsettled state of affairs in this era is found in the account given by Josephus, who says: "When Cyrenius had now disposed of Archelaus's money, and when the taxings were come to a conclusion, which were made in the thirty-seventh year of Ceasar's victory over Antony at Actium, he deprived Joazer of the high priesthood, which dignity had been conferred on him by the multitude, and he appointed Ananus, the son of Seth, to be high priest . . . Valerius Gratus . . . deprived Ananus of the high priesthood, and appointed Ishmael, the son of Phabi, to be priest. He also deprived him in a time, and ordained Eleazer, the son of Ananus, who had been high priest before, to be high priest; which office, when he had held it for a year, Gratus deprived him of, and gave the high priesthood to Simon, son of Camithus, and, when he had possessed that dignity no longer than a year, Joseph Caiaphas was made his successor. When Gratus had done these things, he went back to Rome, after he had tarried in Judea eleven years, when Pontius Pilate came as his successor."

The priesthood had been steered into evil waters. Thus it continued until the time appointed for the consummation of the Jewish state. The Roman army under Titus, encircling the walls of Jerusalem, drew the siege ever tighter, until the city fell in A.D. 70, and with the burning of the temple, altar, sacrifices and priest were taken from Judaism. A new day had dawned for the world, and their refusal to heed "the signs of the times" spelled doom for the Jewish people. A new high priest had been coronated in the heavens, a new mediator had been ushered in by blood. The time of which the prophets had spoken had finally arrived.

THE TIME OF REFORMATION

"According to this arrangement, gifts and sacrifices are offered which cannot perfect the conscience of the worshiper, but deal only with food and drink and various ablutions, regulations for the body imposed until the time of reformation" (Heb. 9: 9, 10). The apostle recognized that the ordinances of the Mosaic economy were only temporary. They constituted restrictions and restraints to hold a people in line until a better covenant based upon better promises could be introduced. That change which then took place involved "a change in the priesthood" and of necessity, "a change in the law as well" (Heb. 7: 12).

Ample warning had been given of God that such a reformation was coming. Jeremiah had declared, "Behold, the days are coming, says the Lord, when I will make a new covenant with the house of Israel and the house of Judah, not like the covenant which I made with their fathers when I took them by the hand to bring them out of the land of Egypt, my covenant which they broke, though I was their husband, says the Lord. But this is the covenant which I will make with the house of Israel, after those days, says the Lord; I will put my law within them, and I will write it upon their hearts; and I will be their God, and they shall be my people. And no longer shall each man teach his neighbor and each his brother, saying, 'Know the Lord,' for they shall all know me, from the least of them, to the greatest, says the Lord" (31: 31-34).

The coming age was to provide new leadership. Ezekiel was told to prophesy against the shepherds of Israel, who were accused of feeding themselves and neglecting the sheep. They were rebuked because they had not strengthened the weak, healed the sick, bound up the crippled, brought back the straying, and sought the lost, but had ruled with force and harshness. God declared, "I will save my flock, they shall no longer be a prey; and I will judge between sheep and sheep. And I will set up over them one shepherd, my servant David, and he shall feed them: he shall feed them and be their shepherd. And I, the Lord, will be their God, and my servant David shall be prince among them; I, the Lord, have spoken. I will make them a covenant of peace and banish wild beasts from the land, so that they may dwell securely in the wilderness and sleep in the woods. And I will make them and the places round about my hill a blessing; and I will send down showers and in their season; they shall be showers of blessing" (Ezekiel 34).

There are numerous allusions in this highly figurative portrayal which should not be overlooked. The exploitation of God's people by their leaders was not to be tolerated. The flock of God was not created to provide food for those who fed them. God said, "Behold, I am against the shepherds; and I will require my sheep at their hand, and put a stop to their feeding the sheep; no longer shall the shepherds feed themselves. I will rescue my sheep from their mouths, that they be not food for them" (Ezek. 33: 10). The shepherds condemned in Ezekiel are "the priests who teach for hire and the prophets who divine for money" as mentioned by Micah (3: 11). Nothing can be clearer than the fact that God intended to wrest his flock from the grasp of mercenaries and hirelings.

This new regime was to be inaugurated when one shepherd was set up over them. The prophet identifies that shepherd as "my servant David." Since David was asleep with his fathers and his sepulcher was with them (Acts 2: 29), when Ezekiel spoke, it is evident that the prophecy pertained to our Lord. Peter declared in the very same connection, "This Jesus God raised up, and of that we are all witnesses" (Acts 2: 32). Accordingly our Lord asserted, "I have other sheep, which are not of this fold; I must bring them also, and they will heed my voice. So there shall be one flock, and one shepherd" (John 10: 16).

The characteristics of the new covenant are set forth. It was to be "a covenant of peace" (Ezek. 34: 25). It was to provide security and safety from harm. Wild beasts were to be banished from the land that the sheep "may dwell securely in the wilderness, and sleep in the woods." It was to secure liberty and freedom. "They shall know that I am the Lord when I break the bars of their yoke, and deliver them from the hand of those who enslave them" (verse 27). The gracious assurance is given, " 'And you are my sheep, the sheep of my pasture, and I am your God', says the Lord God" (verse 31).

The evangelical seer, gazing into the future, and speaking as he was moved by the Holy Spirit, paints an unparalleled picture of the Christian dispensation. The walls of the city of God are to be called "Salvation" and the gates "Praise." The sun will no longer be needed for light by day, nor the moon at night. Instead the Lord will be an everlasting light, and God will be the glory of his people. Jehovah declares, "Your people shall all be righteous; they shall possess the land forever, the shoot of my planting, the work of my hands, that I might be glorified" (Isa. 60: 18-21).

Following this, Isaiah gives that noble declaration of the coming Christ, which Jesus personally read to the synagogue assembled in his home city of Nazareth, and of which he said "Today this scripture has been fulfilled in your hearing" (Isa. 61: 1, 2; Luke 4: 16-21). Then the prophet affirms that those who receive the "good tidings" which the Lord was "anointed to bring" will be called "oaks of righteousness, the planting of the Lord, that he may be glorified." These are destined for a work of restoration (6: 4) and they shall "be called the priests of the Lord, men shall speak of you as the ministers of our God" (Isa. 61:6). "All who see them shall acknowledge them, that they are a people whom the Lord has blessed" (verse 9).

Nothing is clearer than the fact that God's purpose was to make ministry and priesthood co-extensive in "the time of reformation." Every person who accepted the good tidings was to be a priest, every such person was to be a minister. Every priest was such because he ministered; every person was to minister because he was a priest. In priesthood and ministry all were to be of equal rank insofar as liberty, privilege and relationship to God are concerned. God's people were no longer to be a kingdom *with* priests, but a kingdom *of* priests; they were not to be a congregation *with* ministers, but a congregation *of* ministers. Priesthood was to be universal in the kingdom of heaven, ministry was to be mutual and reciprocal. This was to be the grand climax of the ages, the golden era of God's dealings with mankind.

God promised Israel that if they would obey his voice and keep his covenant they would be a kingdom of priests and a holy nation unto him. But they did not obey his voice nor keep his covenant. They never realized the fruition of the magnificent promise because they failed to meet the conditions. But God's purpose was not defeated. He created a new Israel of God (Gal. 6: 16), made up of those who are Christ's, and are Abraham's offspring, and heirs according to promise (Gal. 3: 29). Every one of these is a priest of God. By substituting those who are the children of Abraham by faith for those who were his children by flesh, God at last made every spiritual son of Abraham a priest. At last, every real Jew is a priest. "For he is not a real Jew who is one outwardly, nor is true circumcision something external and physical. He is a Jew who is one inwardly, and real circumcision is a matter of the heart, spiritual and not literal." (Rom. 2: 28, 29).

To effect this great transformation there had to be a new covenant, new altar and new sacrifice. Under the previous covenant only a limited priesthood could obtain. "If perfection had been attainable through the Levitical priesthood what further need would there have been for another priest to arise after the order of Melchizedek, rather than one named after the order of Aaron? For when there is a change in the priesthood, there is necessarily a change in the law as well" (Heb. 7: 11, 12). *There is a change in the priesthood!* These are the words of inspiration. Since "the end of the ages" is come upon us, it is evident that God's plan of priesthood must reach its perfection in this dispensation, or his purpose be forever frustrated. Inasmuch as the latter is an unthinkable conclusion, it is apparent that in the functioning of every child of God as a priest, and only in that way, we see the perfected design of heaven carried out.

The creation of any system which sets up a special class of priestly functionaries to minister in behalf of their fellows in things pertaining to God not only usurps the rights of the remainder of God's priests, but of even greater consequence, it does despite to the Spirit of grace, by introducing again a limited priesthood which can never produce perfection. Such a system has no more place under a faultless covenant than the burning of incense or animal sacrifices. Yet, the ambition of men's hearts for power and prestige is so prevalent, that a constant battle must be waged to keep an indifferent, indolent membership from surrendering their privileges and responsibilities to a group of professional worship directors who sell their talents and abilities for filthy lucre.

Under the Mosaic economy, the priests, and no one else could approach God's sanctuary. Yet those priests must come by the blood of the altar and the laver of baptism in order to enter the tent of meeting. It is still true that only the priests of God can participate in his service. But all who are in his congregation are priests. "Christ appeared once in the end of the age to put away sin by the sacrifice of himself" (Heb. 9: 26). "By a single offering he has perfected for all time those who are sanctified" (Heb. 10: 14). "Therefore, brethren, since we have confidence to enter the sanctuary by the blood of Jesus, by the new and living way which he opened for us through the curtain, that is, through his flesh, and since we have a great priest over the house of God, let us draw near with a true heart in full assurance of faith, with our hearts sprinkled clean from an evil conscience and our bodies washed with pure water" (Heb. 10: 19-22). Every one who has had the blood applied to his heart and who has been immersed in the laver of baptism is a priest with right of entrance into the sanctuary.

In the former dispensation every priest who was consecrated participated in God's service. One could not hire another. It is true that in that imperfect era the congregation could support priests to minister in their behalf, but that was because the congregation was not permitted to minister in the sanctuary. When King Uzziah "was strong he grew proud, to his destruction. For he was false to the Lord his God, and entered the temple of the Lord to burn incense on the altar of incense. But Azariah the priest went in after him, with eighty priests of the Lord who were men of valor, and they withstood King Uzziah, and said to him, 'It is not for you, Uzziah, to burn incense to the Lord, but for the priests the sons of Aaron, who are consecrated to burn incense. Go out of the sanctuary; for you have done wrong, and it will bring you no honor from the Lord God'" (2 Chron. 26: 16-18). Uzziah was stricken with leprosy for his rashness. It is amazing that when men could not be priests they wished to be; and now that they can be they prefer to hire another to minister in their stead.

Even under the law one priest could not hire another. The priests were ordained to serve. Since every Christian is now a priest, it is certainly a travesty upon God's plan for a congregation of priests to hire another priest to minister in their behalf in things pertaining unto God. Such a procedure produces two evils. In the first place, it defeats the very purpose of God as to priesthood by creating a sense of helplessness and dependency upon the part of the greater majority of his priests, and in the second place it creates a professional caste who serve for wages or hire. Thus the birthright of heaven is casually sold by one, and scornfully bought by another. If Simon the Sorcerer was condemned because he thought the gift of God could be *purchased for money,* what will be the fate of those who think it can be *sold for money?*

There is no priesthood in God's program now but that which is common to all Christians. That which makes one a Christian makes him a priest of God. The literal priesthood has been supplanted by the spiritual; the limited has been succeeded by the universal. Yet the religious world has been captivated by a special clergy. Designate it what you will, this is but a limited priesthood, arrogating to itself those rights which belong to all. Nothing is more certain than the fact that the average religionist believes that this special group of ministerial functionaries is a product of New Testament teaching. Yet it is apparent that the system which produces them is a denial of the very essence of the New Covenant and an espousal of the program of the Old Covenant. Those who seek justification for a special priesthood in this dispensation are also seeking to be justified by the law and are fallen from grace.

The time of reformation has come. It has brought with it certain changes. Those changes must be recognized. To deny them or abrogate them is to flout God's purpose.

1. There has been a change of sacrifice. The animal sacrifices once required are no longer demanded. To offer such sacrifices now would be to crucify the Son of God afresh and put him to an open shame.

2. There has been a change of law. No longer are we subject to the "regulations for worship in the earthly sanctuary" (Heb. 9: 1). The law had "but a shadow of the good things to come instead of the true form of these realities" (Heb. 10: 1). The man who chooses to be justified by the law shows a preference for the shadow rather than the reality.

3. There has been a change of priesthood. The

limited has given way to the universal. With the introduction of the priesthood of all believers, no particular class or caste has an exclusive right "to perform ritual duties." Indeed it is one of the absolute essentials to priesthood that each person who is a priest "have something to offer" (Heb. 8: 3). The change in the priesthood has conferred upon all of God's priests the right to minister unto God subject to the restrictions of the Great King.

This great truth was recognized in the primitive church. "The devotional exercises of the Christian assemblies, like those of the Jewish synagogues, consisted principally of prayers, singing of hymns, and sacred discourses, founded upon positions of the Old Testament. Apostolic epistles were read in the congregation, to which they had been generally directed, but after a single reading they were generally laid aside. Every one who had power and the inclination to speak in public was allowed to do so with freedom" (*A History of the Christian Church,* by Dr. Charles Hase. Pages 40, 41).

The mystery of iniquity which began to work even during apostolic days soon changed this state of affairs, and wrested the rights from the many and gave them into the hands of the powerful few. This was done by recourse to the limited priesthood of the law as a pattern. Writing about conditions in the second century, our same learned historian, who was Professor of Theology in the University of Jena, says: "The offices of the Church at this period presented very little to excite the cupidity of ordinary men, and even the honor attending them was counterbalanced by the dangers. And yet it seemed desirable to increase the veneration which necessarily attends the virtues and a faithful performance of official duty in the Church, by mysterious forms of ordination, *by connecting them through various associations with the Old Testament priesthood,* and by external tokens of peculiar sanctity. The result was that even in the second century the priests (Kleros) were represented as the official mediators between Christ and the congregation (Laos). To speak in the church, and to administer holy rites, were conceded to be the special prerogatives of the clergy, although learned laymen were sometimes heard in the public assembly, with the consent of the bishop. In all things relating to the business of the congregation, the principal care and authority devolved upon the clergy, but this power was generally exercised mildly and with a true regard for the public good, since those who possessed it could use no external means of coercion, and the clergy, being generally *without fixed salaries, were dependent upon the voluntary contributions of the people.* Their authority was often much straitened by the influence of the confessors, and *the idea was not yet removed of a priesthood embracing all true Christians*" (Ibid., pp. 57, 58).

From the foregoing, it is apparent that one of the first steps to the formation of a special clergy was the denial of the freedom to every one who had the power and inclination to speak in public. Although, for prestige and pride a learned layman was sometimes given the privilege of being heard in the public assembly, "to speak in the church was conceded to be the prerogative of the clergy." Yet, the rise of the clergy to dominant power was temporarily restrained by the fact that they were generally without stipulated salaries, and dependent upon voluntary contributions; as well as by the lingering concept of a priesthood of all believers. However, the surrender of the freedom to address the brethren by those who had the ability and desire to do it, into the hands of a special group of ministrants, was the seed from which the clergy sprung, and soon the guaranteed wage for serving God in behalf of men was introduced, and with it passed away the real function of the priesthood of all believers, and a *limited priesthood* once more came into vogue. It is not amiss to state that the clergy system and the financial guarantee always go hand in hand.

When the members of the church become so indolent and wrapped up with worldliness that they no longer study the holy scriptures, when they become so indifferent to the needs of their brethren that they no longer seek to excel to the edifying of the church, when freedom means so little that they will gladly surrender it to pamper pride, they begin automatically to try and purchase that for which they are not willing to exert personal effort. And when men demand professional ministers there will arise professional ministers to supply the demand. However, a system of universal priesthood can no more exist side by side with a system of limited priesthood, than we can be under the reign of grace and the Mosaic law at the same time. The professional ministry with its contracts to men cannot exist side by side with the mutual ministry growing out of a covenant with God.

We are living in "the time of reformation" of which the prophet spoke. The "end of the ages" has come. God's great ideal must reach its culmination in our lives. It is not for us to question whether his plan will work. It is but for us to work his plan. It is not for us to seek to improve upon his design or pattern, or through fear to shape, trim and alter it to meet our ideas, but to restore that pattern, firm in the conviction that he "who does not slumber nor sleep" will not fail us, but will attend us in our way.

At the root of almost every departure and apostasy is the pride of men. We are more afraid of what men will think about us than we are of what God thinks. We want to make a show, a demonstration, a manifestation of power, ability, and wealth. We worship culture and kneel as abject slaves at the shrine of conformity. The simple worship of the saints around the festal board has become a well-planned pageant, in which immaculate actors carry out a rigid formal ritual. The speaker's platform is not a stand in which humble farmers, mechanics or carpenters may exhort their fellow Christians to endure trials, overcome temptations and grow in grace, but it is a carpeted stage on which a polished performer presents a perfected oration for which he has been personally prepared. We are more concerned about what our worldly friends think of "our minister" than we are as to what they think of God's Son. God's time of reformation is here; it is now time that our reformation begin.

THE ORDER OF MELCHIZEDEK

No study of the priesthood as set forth in the New Covenant would be complete without a knowledge of the high priesthood of Christ from which it stems, and no investigation of the priesthood of God's Messiah can afford to ignore the order upon which it is based. After Melchizedek appeared briefly on the scene of God's history in the days of Abraham, he disappeared without further mention until David records the words of God declaring that he would make his Son "a priest for ever, after the order of Melchizedek" (Psalm 110: 4). Accordingly, when the writer of Hebrews desired to emphasize the superiority of the New Covenant to the Old Covenant, he had recourse to the diversity in the priesthoods of these respective revelations. He cites the prediction of David and directly applies it to the Son of God (Heb. 5: 6).

In conjunction with the statement that Christ was "designated by God a high priest after the order of Melchizedek" he continues, "About this we have much to say which is hard to explain, since you have become dull of hearing" (Heb. 5: 11). This indicates that it is a difficult task to expound the truths concerning the priesthood of Christ to those whose hearing has become dull. The original word for "dull" means "lazy, sluggish, indolent, stupid." The word for "hearing" relates to the ability to perceive truth or grasp the force of reasoning. The occasion of the dullness of the Hebrews is assigned to the fact that they have not had "their faculties trained by practice to distinguish good from evil." The result was that at the time when they should have been teachers they required someone to teach them again the first principles of God's Word.

We face today the same difficulty as did the writer of the Hebrew letter. The subject of God's priesthood falls upon ears that are dulled by inattention, traditionalism and prejudice. The average member of the church does not have his faculties trained to distinguish good from evil. Men, who long ago should have become teachers, must still have rudimentary principles explained to them over and over again. There is no limitation of the Holy Spirit's ability to explain, the limitation is upon the part of man to grasp. The limitation could be removed by the diligent application of the faculties through study. Trained faculties like trained soldiers are not produced by merely hearing textual lectures.

The inspired writer, although recognizing the difficulty did not demur from the task of explaining God's system of priesthood, and no more should we be discouraged by a kindred problem. Like him, we also should "desire each one of you to show the same earnestness in realizing the full assurance of hope until the end, *so that you may not be sluggish,* but imitators of those who through faith and patience inherit the promises" (Heb. 6: 11, 12). We shall proceed to an investigation of the order under which the priesthood of Christ was inaugurated. This will necessitate a careful study of Hebrews, chapter seven.

In this chapter, there are a number of valid arguments introduced to establish the priesthood of Christ over that of the Levitical priests. The principal arguments are drawn from the following considerations:

1. Melchizedek was both king and priest, and his superiority in rank was acknowledged even by Abraham, the father of the Jewish race. Thus Levi who had not yet been born, could be said to have acknowledged this superiority representatively through his illustrious ancestor, who paid tithes to Melchizedek.

2. Perfection was not attainable through the Levitical priesthood (verse 11) because "the law made nothing perfect" (verse 19). With the abrogation of the law because of its weakness and uselessness (verse 18) the better hope is introduced by which we draw nigh to God (verse 19) and the priesthood thus created would be superior to one based upon a law which could make nothing perfect.

3. The priesthood of the Old Covenant was not constituted with a solemn oath of God, but the priesthood of Jesus began in this august fashion. "This makes Jesus the surety of a better covenant" (verse 22).

4. The tenure in office of the former priests was uncertain and discontinued by death, making succession an imperative to the perpetuity of the system. In the case of our Lord a permanent, unchangeable priesthood is assured because he always lives to make intercession.

5. The priests of old were frail, weak, and sinful creatures, who had first to offer sacrifices for their own sins, before they could minister in behalf of the congregation. Our high priest is "holy, blameless, unstained, separated from sinners and exalted above the heavens" (verse 26) and is superior in nature, character and attributes to those of the previous dispensation.

FACTS ABOUT MELCHIZEDEK

Verse 1. His name Melchizedek means "king of righteousness." He was also king of Salem (Jerusalem) which word means "peace." He met Abraham returning from the slaughter of the kings and blessed him, as also recorded in Genesis 14: 14-20.

Verse 2. Abraham apportioned to Melchizedek a tenth part of everything. This was done out of respect for the superior office of this man, and perhaps as an expression of thanksgiving unto God for the satisfactory culmination of the battle to rescue Lot and his goods, since Abraham recognized Melchizedek as a priest of God Most High.

Verse 3. Melchizedek is said to be "without father or mother or genealogy." This does not mean that he literally had no parents. The subject under consideration is the priestly function. No one was allowed to serve in the Jewish priesthood unless he could "trace his title clear" in the carefully guarded genealogical records (Cp. Ezra 2: 62). We know the father of Aaron was Amram, and his mother was Jochebed. The record has preserved their names. We know that the sons of Aaron were Nadab, Abihu, Eleazar, and Ithamar. But no one knows the name of the father, or mother, or posterity of Melchizedek, because the record is silent on these matters.

The expression that he "has neither beginning of days nor end of life" means simply that we have no historical record of his birth or death, or of the beginning or conclusion of his priestly office. The Jewish readers were ever anxious to trace *from the record* the cessation of a man's priesthood, and determine his successor. But so far as the record is concerned one can determine no end to the priesthood of Melchizedek, and on that basis and as far as the record goes, that priesthood is continuous. No man can produce the record of its culmination.

It is affirmed that "resembling the Son of God he continues a priest for ever." This does not mean we cannot trace the literal genealogy of Jesus, because we have two accounts given of it (Matt. 1 and Luke 3) but he had no genealogical record *as a priest* such as the Jews required, and indeed his literal genealogical record showing he came from Judah would have made it impossible for him to be a priest on earth (Heb. 8: 4).

Melchizedek and Jesus resembled in the fact that each was a king as well as a priest; each was a king of righteousness and a prince of peace; neither had direct ancestors or successors in the priestly office and so far as the record shows both continued in office: Melchizedek because the record gives no account of his death; Jesus because the record attests that "he always lives."

Verse 4. Abraham is designated "the patriarch" which means "chief father." In the reasoning of the Jews he would be superior in rank to any of his posterity, which would include the sons of Levi. Yet Abraham recognized the superior dignity of Melchizedek and manifested it by voluntarily conferring upon him a tenth of the booty taken in his foray against the retreating invaders.

Verse 5. Not all of Levi's descendants were priests, but those who did receive the priestly office were by the law commissioned to receive tithes from their brethren, as a recognition of the dignity of the office.

Verses 6, 7. Melchizedek who was not in the genealogy of Levi not only received tithes from the eminent father of the Jewish nation, but also blessed Abraham who had the promises. Since "it is beyond dispute that the inferior is blessed by the superior," these two items—the tithes bestowed *by* Abraham and the blessing bestowed *upon* Abraham—prove that Melchizedek was superior in rank not only to Abraham, but to any of his descendants in the flesh, none of whom could outrank their father.

Verse 8. The Levitical priests who received tithes soon had to forfeit their office, because they were mortal, and the record of their deaths is proof of the need of successors, but nowhere does *the record* indicate the cessation of the office of Melchizedek who took a tenth of the spoils from Abraham.

Verses 9, 10. Although Abraham, as patriarch, had the promises, he recognized the superiority of Melchizedek in his priestly office. He stood as a representative of that nation which would proceed from his loins, and the inspired writer points out the consequence of his voluntary act of deference. Although Levi had not yet been born, through Abraham his progenitor, it was as if he too paid tithes to Melchizedek, thus establishing the great fact that those mortal men who received tithes under the law were inferior to him who prior to the law was both king and priest. So the priesthood of the order of Aaron must be considered as inferior to that of the order of Melchizedek.

THE WEAKNESS OF THE LAW

Verse 11. The Jews regarded their legal system as perfect and permanent. They reasoned that inasmuch as it had been personally announced by Jehovah under awe-inspiring conditions at Sinai, he would not repudiate his covenant. They overlooked the apparent fact that they had themselves nullified it by their disobedience. But that it could not produce perfection is here shown from the fact that if it did this would render unnecessary the coming of another priest who was not after the order of Aaron, which order was recognized and created by that law. Yet that another priest after another order must arise was attested to by the patriarch David in Psalm 110: 4. Since a new priesthood could not improve on that which was already perfect, the necessity of a new one arising argued the weakness and imperfection of the one then in existence.

Verse 12. This verse renders a death blow to those who contend that we are still under the law given at Sinai. We cannot be under the priesthood of Christ and the law of Moses. If we are not under the priesthood of Christ, we are still under the law requiring animal sacrifices. If we are not under that law we are under a different priesthood than the one which that law produced.

Verses 13, 14. The argument of the inspired writer is clinched by the fact that Christ was not of the tribe of Levi, but of the tribe of Judah, in connection with which Moses said nothing about priests. If perfection were by the Mosaic law, it would be achieved under the Levitical priesthood. That it could not be so secured is evidenced from the prophecy that another priesthood would be inaugurated, and the one who became high priest under the new regime would be from a different tribe than the one authorized by law to furnish priests.

Verses 15, 16, 17. Our Lord became a priest "by the power of an indestructible life," and not as did the former priests "according to a legal requirement concerning bodily descent." The priests of the Mosaic dispensation were not inducted into their high office as a result of a proven character or guileless conduct. They were born into a certain family, and by virtue of legislation regarding that fleshly descent they became priests. The priesthood of Christ is more spiritual in nature, and is enduring and perpetual, being in that respect far superior to the Levitical priesthood.

Verses 18, 19. The former commandment was set aside because of its weakness and unprofitableness to secure the final great purpose of God, the salvation of man. The law answered the purpose for which it was intended, as "a custodian until Christ came" (Gal. 3: 24). It was designed for that, and having been added because of transgression until the seed came, it did all it was intended to do. It was given to a limited number, for a limited purpose and a limited time.

The law could not produce perfection (verse 11), nor purge the conscience from dead works, nor could it expiate sin. It was removed that a better hope could be introduced, by which we draw nigh to God. With such a high priest as we now have we can draw near with true hearts in full assurance of hope.

THE OATH OF OFFICE

Verses 20, 21, 22. The third link in the chain of argument designed to prove the superiority of the Messianic priesthood over that of Aaron is the fact that Christ was confirmed in his office by an oath of God, whereas the former priests were inducted with appropriate ritualism upon the basis of mere legislative arrangement. When the time came for Aaron and his sons to be ordained, Moses was given simple and detailed instructions as to the consecration ceremonies. There was no extraordinary proceeding as may be seen by examination of the events described in Exodus 28.

In the case of Christ, the Father declared with a solemn oath that the Son would be a priest for ever. Those who are sufficiently interested in the scriptural research necessary to determine the occasions upon which God employed an oath to confirm his word, will find that God never took such a solemn step unless he wanted to manifest the absolute certainty and immutability of his decrees. God's promise does not require an oath to make it binding. He will as readily fulfill his word unaccompanied by an oath, as he will that word attested by swearing an oath. But in matters of the gravest importance God employs an oath for our benefit. It is accepted universally among men that the highest form of attestation is by oath. "Men indeed swear by a greater than themselves, and in all their disputes an oath is final for confirmation. So when God desired to show more convincingly to the heirs of the promise the unchangeable character of his purpose, he interposed with an oath" (Heb. 6: 16, 17).

Since God employs an oath to demonstrate the unalterable character of his purpose, the fact that the Levitical priesthood was inaugurated without an oath is an argument that it could well be recognized as temporary and impermanent. The reverse is true concerning the priesthood of Christ relative to which it is affirmed, "God hath sworn and will not repent." When man repents he changes his will; when God repents he wills a change. No change will be made in the present system of priesthood. It will never be superseded by another. So long as the priestly relationship is demanded in approach to God, it will be sustained in Christ Jesus. He will have no successor to his office.

The inspired writer declares that "this makes Jesus the surety of a better covenant." The word "surety" is from the Greek *egguos,* and is nowhere else used in the New Testament, nor in the Septuagint. We cannot therefore arrive at its meaning by observing its usage by inspired writers. It is quite common in classic Greek, where it means "a bondsman or sponsor." It refers to one who pledges his property, his social standing, or his sacred honor that a certain thing will be carried out. If a man is apprehended by the law, he must give some assurance that he will appear in court. He is said to be "released on bond." The one who deposits the amount of money, securities or other negotiable interests to guarantee the appearance of the one arrested is called "the bondsman or surety." When one borrows money from a bank he must secure the name of other property owners as *surety*. Those who co-sign the note guarantee the payment of the borrowed sum.

Jesus, by virtue of his office and the oath which confirmed it unto him, is our surety of a better covenant based upon better promises (Heb. 8: 6). His sacrifice and death attest unto us that all of the promises of God will be fulfilled. His resurrection from the dead is a guarantee that "he who raised Christ Jesus from the dead will give life to your mortal bodies also through his Spirit which dwells in you" (Rom. 7: 11). His present position as mediator and high priest in our behalf is a token that we may "with confidence draw near to the throne of grace" (Heb. 4: 16).

THE PERMANENT PRIESTHOOD

Verses 23, 24, 25. The argument for superiority as made in this section of Hebrews 7, is based upon the plurality of priests occasioned by death under the former dispensation, and the singularity and permanency of the priesthood of Christ Jesus.

The former priests were many in number, because of human frailty and mortality. Regardless of how excellent they might be in personal conduct, or how efficient in administration of ritual duties, death took its toll. From the time that the mantle was taken from the shoulders of Aaron and placed upon Eleazar until A.D. 70 when Phannias served as the final high priest, eighty-one men in order had ministered in the holy place. This is a sufficient commentary on the inspired statement "they were prevented by death from continuing in office."

How different it is with our Lord. "He holds his priesthood permanently, because he continues for ever." He has conquered death, and it holds no terrors for him. He is victor over it, and it cannot engulf him as it did the former priests. The superiority of his priesthood over theirs is as great as that of life over death, as immortality. He will not relinquish the priestly mitre to another brow. Upon the peaks of Mount Hor, "Moses stripped Aaron of his garments, and put them upon Eleazar his son; and Aaron died there on the top of the mountain" (Num. 20: 28). No such scene will ever occur in the career of our great high priest.

The consoling thought to us is that "he is able for all time to save those who draw near to God through him, since he always lives to make intercession for them." Man must draw near to God. He must do this through Christ. All who thus draw near he is able to save, and to do it for all time. This ability comes from the fact that he always lives to make intercession. He need not begin his work only to be forced to relinquish it to another. His ability is not circumscribed by liability to failure through death or deposition from office.

THE SINLESS CHARACTER

Verses 26, 27, 28. The final argument is based upon the spotless nature and unsullied character of Christ Jesus as contrasted with the sinful nature of the former priests who had to offer sacrifices in their behalf.

In view of the fact that we constitute "a holy priesthood, to offer up spiritual sacrifices acceptable to God through Jesus Christ" (1 Pet. 2: 5), "it was fitting that we should have such a high priest, holy, blameless, unstained, separated from sinners, exalted above the heavens." He is separated from sinners in that he did not partake of their sins, enter into their plans, or succumb to their temptations. He was not segregated from them while on earth, for it was charged that "this man eateth with publicans and sinners," but his association with them was not to indulge in their carnal pleasures but to lead them into a purer life. Physically, he moved among them for their good; spiritually, he was separated from them lest he be evil. His present exalted position at the right hand of God enables him to further the work of intercession which he ever carries on in our behalf.

He has no need to offer sacrifices daily as did the former priests. Nor did he ever require a sin offering in his own behalf. He offered himself once for all and thus culminated sin offerings. Is this not a refutation of the doctrine of the Roman Catholic mass which is claimed by a deceiving priestcraft to be a daily sacrifice?

Answering the question, "What do you mean by the mass?" Conway says, "The mass, according to Catholic doctrine, is a commemoration of the sacrifice of the cross, for as often as we celebrate it, we show the death of the Lord until he come (1 Cor. 11: 16). At the same time, it is not a bare commemoration of that other sacrifice, since it is also itself a true sacrifice because it has all the essentials of a true sacrifice: its Priest, Jesus Christ, using the ministry of an earthly representative; its victim, Jesus Christ, truly present under the appearance of bread and wine; its sacrificial offerings, the mystic rite of consecration." Again, "Catholics hold that the infinite merits and efficacy of the sacrifice of the cross cannot be increased by any new sacrifice. The mass is not a new sacrifice, but the continuation of the bloody sacrifice of the cross applied in an unbloody manner to the souls of individual Christians."

If Jesus is a priest, and his body the victim, and he daily engages in its sacrificial offering, the Scriptures are at fault in declaring, "He entered once for all into the Holy Place, taking not the blood of goats and calves but his own blood, thus securing an eternal redemption" (Heb. 9: 12). What can be plainer than the following? "Nor was it to offer himself repeatedly, as the high priest enters the Holy Place yearly with blood not his own; for then he would have had to suffer repeatedly, since the foundation of the world. But as it is, he has appeared once for all at the end of the age to put away sin by the sacrifice of himself" (Heb. 9: 25, 26).

The *priestcraft* of Rome stands out here in direct contrast to the priesthood of heaven. In order to lend power to a human system, Rome changed the table of God into an altar, the supper into a sacrifice, the emblems into a victim. No longer could the communicants gather as a family around the household thanksgiving table; instead they must prostrate themselves as supplicants before an altar. And as altars and sacrifices must have their priests, so the hierarchy moved in to supply the daily need—always for the necessary remuneration, of course. How gladly should we receive the good news that "we have been sanctified through the offering of the body of Jesus Christ once for all" (Heb. 10:10).

THE ROYAL PRIESTHOOD

The ideal of God for a kingdom composed entirely of priests is achieved in the relationship created by the new covenant. That which could not be accomplished at Mount Sinai has been accomplished at Mount Sion, where we received a kingdom which cannot be moved or shaken. Every child of God is a priest, every one is now a minister.

In the Revelation letter John informs us of Jesus "who loves us and has freed us from our sins by his blood and made us a kingdom, priests to his God and Father" (Rev. 1: 5, 6). This one statement tells us of the motivation (love), the action (freed us), and the means (his blood), by which Jesus achieved his goal of founding a unique kingdom.

Because of the priestly nature of the kingdom, celestial voices are raised in this hymn of praise:

"Worthy art thou to take the scroll
and to open its seals,
For thou wast slain and by thy blood
didst redeem men for God
From every tribe and tongue and people
and nation,
And hast made them a kingdom and priests
to our God" (Revelation 5: 9, 10).

Let us examine the language of the Spirit. The terms "high priest" and "chief priest" are found 123 times in the new covenant scriptures. Of these occurrences, 113 directly or indirectly refer to the high priests or chief priests of Judaism.

The ten exceptions are all located in the epistle to the Hebrews and are direct references to our Lord Jesus Christ. They present him as the great high priest who was foreshadowed by the high priests under the law of Moses. Accordingly, there is not a hint in these occurrences of any priest in the kingdom of God, except our Lord himself.

The Greek word for priest is *hiereus.* The term "priest" is found 33 times in the new covenant scriptures. It refers to the Levitical priests 18 times. Of the fifteen remaining occurrences, 8 refer to Christ, 3 to Melchizedek, 1 to the pagan priest of Jupiter, and the other 3 to the entire membership of the community of saints, who are described as "a kingdom, even priests."

The word "priest" is never once applied to a special ministry or caste in the congregation of our Lord. No gospel preacher, bishop, or deacon, was ever referred to as a priest in any distinctive sense; no such individual was a priest by right of office.

The word "priesthood" is found but six times in the new covenant scriptures. Four of these appearances are in one chapter (Hebrews 7). In every instance the four refer either to the Levitical priesthood or to that of our Lord. The other two instances are also found in one chapter. They designate the entire body of believers as "a holy priesthood" (1 Peter 2: 5), and "a royal priesthood" (1 Peter 2: 9).

Nothing is clearer than the fact that in the primitive Christian community there was no priesthood other than that of the Lord Jesus Christ and every one of his followers, who were to "offer up spiritual sacrifices acceptable unto God." The special priesthood which is so prevalent in our day has no scriptural precedent under the rule of Jesus. It has been created by men and has arisen without divine warrant. It usurps the privileges and prerogatives which belong to all alike. It makes a pretentious claim to authority but it asserts a divine right without a word of divine writ to sustain it. God's magnificent plan for the ages culminates in every saint recognized as a real priest. Any attempt to promote a special priesthood clothed with special powers to minister in things pertaining unto God thwarts the divine purpose. It exists as an affront to the Great King and his humble and loyal subjects.

In spite of this we are faced with the fact that in our day the idea of a special priesthood to minister for and in behalf of other saints is so prevalent that a majority of believers have no concept of the people of God functioning in any other manner. Few indeed realize that they were ever intended to be priests, and their idea of priesthood has been so conditioned by the subservient role to which they are reconciled that they find it ludicrous to consider themselves as priests in any sense.

The danger of this lies in the fact that the kingdom of heaven is designed to be a kingdom of priests. It derives its nature from a citizenry composed of priests. If we create a wholly different order in which the citizens disclaim any relationship as priests, there is a question as to whether it can be regarded as the kingdom of heaven or not. To what extent can we alter the fundamental constituency of the kingdom of heaven and still regard ourselves as composing it? Perhaps nothing is more important for our generation than a recapture of the royal priesthood.

This brings us to the place where we may well investigate another word—*clergy*. It is from the Greek *kleeros* which means "a lot, an inheritance." In the original it occurs thirteen times in the Scriptures. It is rendered heritage 1, inheritance 2, lot 3, lots 5, and part 2 times. The word is never used to mark off a segment or portion of God's people from the rest in the new covenant scriptures. All who have been redeemed and have entered into Christ constitute the heritage of God. He has not selected a special group to serve as his lot or inheritance.

This was not true under the legalistic regime created by the old covenant. Then God had a special inheritance, a clergy to act as his special functionaries. "At that time the Lord set apart the tribe of Levi, to carry the ark of the covenant of the Lord, to stand before the Lord to minister to him, and to bless in his name to this day. Therefore Levi has no *portion* or *inheritance* with his brothers; the Lord is his *inheritance,* as the Lord your God said to him" (Deuteronomy 10: 8, 9).

Observe that here a special group was set apart, or ordained to minister unto God and to pronounce a blessing or benediction upon the remainder of the congregation in God's name. Under Judaism there was a distinction between the clergy and the laity. There were certain rituals reserved exclusively for the priests, or clergy, to perform. The people were not permitted to enter the sacred areas or to engage in the clerical functions.

Inasmuch as the Levitical priests constituted a special clergy to minister unto God, they were to be supported in their clerical duties by those in whose behalf they ministered. "The Levitical priests, that is all the tribe of Levi, shall have no portion or inheritance with Israel; they shall eat the offerings by fire to the Lord, and his rightful dues. They shall have no inheritance among their brethren; the Lord is their *inheritance* as he promised them" (Deuteronomy 18: 1, 2).

Nothing is clearer than the fact that under "the ministration of death" which was written and engraven in stones God created a clergy with certain sacerdotal functions. Those who composed it wore distinctive robes and stood between the people and God. But all such distinctions were rendered invalid by the cross of Christ.

We are not under law, but under grace. "The law came by Moses, but grace and truth came by Jesus Christ." We are under a better covenant based upon better promises. Under the reign of grace God no longer has a special tribe ordained as clergymen. Through grace every child of God is sanctified and anointed, set apart and ordained to offer spiritual sacrifices acceptable unto him. We are all God's portion or inheritance in the world.

Every Christian is a clergyman in the only scriptural usage of the term. To create a special clergy is to lapse back into Judaism. It is easier to live under law than under grace. Law creates its special interpreters and judges, and the community can rest in their judgment and be relieved of personal responsibility. When problems arise men can "go up to the priest," and his clerical interpretation becomes the authorized guide. Yet it was from this very system Jesus died to deliver us. He made us free from all priestly and hierarchical domination.

It is impossible to create a special clergy without, by the same act, creating *a laity*. The word *laos* from which we get "laity" is found at least 141 times in the new covenant scriptures, where it is translated "people."

In every instance when applied to the community of Christ it refers to the whole body of believers. It never refers to a group as distinguished from a priestly or ministerial class. This was not true under the legalistic covenant. There was always a careful line of distinction drawn between the priests (clergy) and the people (laity).

"And he (the high priest) shall make atonement for the priests (clergy) and for all the people (laity) of the assembly" (Leviticus 16: 33). "These preparations having thus been made, the priests (clergy) go continually into the outer tent, performing their ritual duties; but into the second only the high priest goes, and he but once a year, and not without taking blood which he offers for himself and for the errors of the people (laity)" (Hebrews 9: 6, 7).

The great difference under the new covenant is illustrated in one important verse. It affirms the priesthood of all believers and uses the term *laos* to designate the same group. "But you are a chosen race, a royal priesthood, a holy nation, God's own people (laity), that you may declare the wonderful deeds of him who called you out of darkness into his marevlous light" (1 Peter 2: 9).

This is a significant passage because it identifies the royal priesthood with God's laity. Every priest of God is one of his laity, every member of God's laity is a priest. Every child of God is his lot or inheritance through the blood of Jesus, therefore, all of God's children constitute his *clergy*. Since they also constitute his *laity*, there can be no distinction between clergy and laity in the kingdom of Christ.

It is worth noting that Peter declares that Christians are God's laity (people), "that you may declare the wonderful deeds of him who called you out of darkness." God's laity are not those to whom messages of God are brought. They are themselves the bringers of a message. The laity are not those who listen to a clergy declare the wonderful works of God; they are the clergy who do the declaring.

It is sad indeed to contemplate how far we have fallen away from God's ideal of the priestly citizenry. It is not uncommon to hear Christians excuse themselves for their ignorance or apathy with the words, "After all, I am just a layman." This is equivalent to saying "I am just one of God's people." The tragedy is that those who thus speak proceed to act as if they are not God's people.

The clergy are expected to engage in religious activities, to walk circumspectly, to employ proper language, to visit the sick and to study the Bible. This is regarded as the field of clerical function. This is what the clergy is paid to do. Those who are "just laymen" live on a different plane. Their function is to go listen to the clergyman and pay his salary for performing a priestly role. But all of this is as far from God's program for the Christian life as the blood of Christ is from the blood of bulls and goats.

Just as any attempt to create a special clergy must result in a laity, so any attempt to create a distinctive laity must result in a special clergy. Sometimes men seek to avoid the implications of their philosophy by employing other terms to designate what they create. They frequently borrow scriptural terminology in the vain hope that a thing may be sanctified by calling a good name over it.

But we may designate the clergy system by whatever terms we will, borrowing the language of apostate ecclesiasticism, or "stealing the livery of heaven" in which to clothe it, yet the fact is that so long as the idea of a special ministerial caste exists, and the remainder of the saints are regarded as "the laity," that long we are nearer to Rome than to Jerusalem. And that long we are standing at a mount that can be touched rather than before Mount Sion.

Let us be very plain so there can be no ground for misunderstanding. We may call our clergyman "our minister," "local evangelist," or just plain "preacher," but if he occupies a place of prominence in the assembly of saints as the front man for the congregation, if he is the exclusive minister, by virtue of his office, "to declare the wonderful works of God," when the whole community come together in one place, and if other saints are excluded from the opportunity by his very presence, we have a special clergyman. A preacher can be a clergyman as easily as a clergyman can be a preacher.

It is going to be very difficult to recover the abandoned ideal of the universal priesthood of believers. This is true for several reasons. The greatest deterrent is the bitter opposition to it by many who profess to be followers of Jesus. We have converted men to systems, structures and organizations. They have no real sense of vital relationship to Jesus as the head of a living organism. They are often lazy, indifferent and unconcerned. And many who never thought of fighting the devil will fight the thought of returning to the responsible role of priesthood. Too, we have been betrayed into measuring spiritual growth by numerical statistics. We have two criteria by which to judge our success—attendance and contributions. This may well be called "the scholar-dollar" fallacy. It operates on the assumption that the greater the number in Sunday School and the greater the bank account the closer to heaven we are. Actually there may be little relationship between the number of dollars in the bank and the number of names in the Book of Life.

To abandon the clergy-oriented modern institution for the Spirit-filled community of saints in the first century is the last thing most people will consider. It is probable that the primitive community was more adapted to meaningful meetings in small homes, third floor walk-up tenements (as at Troas), or in catacombs and caves. Here those who were fighting for survival of a cause could come and bind up their wounds, share their experiences and exhort one another to shoulder the cross again. Their problem was not the institutional community image but how to survive individually until the morrow.

We must be realistic enough to recognize that we live in a modern world. There are many conditions in twentieth century America which were undreamed of in first century Palestine or Asia Minor. Religion has been institutionalized for many centuries. Millions who want to follow Jesus do not think of themselves as runners, pugilists or soldiers in a spiritual sense. References to such activities are regarded as portraying a quaint symbolism of a bygone area.

We are resigned to being spectators rather than participants. The action is to be carried out by trained professionals. We are the drama critics who sit in favored locations and observe the presentation without ever becoming really involved. We are like natives watching a battle from the hills whose special interests favor one side in the conflict, but who never move down into the fray.

It is evident that a priestly role involves service to God. A priest under the old covenant did not act by proxy. He was not a mere onlooker but an active sharer in the responsibilities pertaining to the temple. But this was only a step in the divine program which was to culminate in a universal priesthood of all believers.

Our tragedy is that we have been betrayed into going back to before the cross and reinstating the concept of priesthood which was a part of Judaism. We have again created a professional priesthood to minister in our behalf. We think of the pulpit as "a holy place" in "the sanctuary" where only those with special ordination or anointing may officiate.

In many cases those who enter the pulpit wear robes to distinguish them from the rest of the saints. They regard the speaker's stand as a "sacred desk" and pronouncements made from it may be uttered in a special "religious voice" adopted for the occasion. Such utterances may be given greater attention than those made by a public schoolteacher who instructs a group of students in a Sunday school class.

The minister may develop a sense of importance as to his position and speak about "my elders," "my church," "my laymen." If he ever regards the body of believers as constituting a priesthood he regards himself as a sort of local high priest whose task is to correlate and be responsible for a ritual or liturgy by which men approach God through his leading or direction. This has tended to institutionalize the church and to eliminate the family feeling so essential to the maintenance of brotherly love under the fatherhood of God.

From time to time there have been movements sparked in the history of the Christian community to get rid of the clergy. John Milton led such an attempt in his day and directed a vitriolic attack. Unfortunately most of these ventures were as negative as they were antagonistic. They were anti-clerical and were directed toward the goal of reducing the clerics to what is called lay-status.

It would seem that a reverse approach would be more in keeping with God's purpose. Those who think of themselves as "the laity" should be taught to regard themselves as "priests of the most high God," and should be equipped for the fulfillment of the priestly function required by the new covenant.

We must come to recognize that God's only sanctuary is the human heart consecrated and dedicated to the high calling of Christian service. In the economy of Christ, priest and sacrifice become one. Jesus offered himself, and it is written, "we are sanctified through the offering of the body of Jesus Christ once for all" (Heb. 10: 10). As a part of the priesthood inaugurated through this universal sacrifice we also must "present our bodies a living sacrifice, holy, acceptable unto God, as a spiritual service."

Unfortunately, we have been betrayed into erecting temples and tabernacles in which we dedicate sanctuaries, and we tend to think of what we do in such special places as service to God. But all of this is pre-Christian and Judaistic in origin. It actually nullifies the power of the cross, while pampering our pride and salving the conscience. Temples require special priests, vestments, liturgies, orders of service, and a great many other things wholly unknown to the new covenant. We have actually forsaken "the order of Melchizedek" for that of Aaron and Levi, and have reverted to "the law of a carnal commandment" in preference to "the power of an endless life" (Hebrews 7: 16).

This does not mean that members of the royal priesthood should not assemble together. Indeed, the very epistle which says the most about priesthood specifically says we should not forsake the assembling of ourselves together. But the same passage tells us that the purpose of our convening should be to incite one another to love and to good works, and to encourage one another (Hebrews 10: 24, 25). We do not meet to conduct a service to God, or to offer a ritualistic sacrifice. We are the sacrifice.

This means that wherever a child of God is, there God is in his sanctuary. If one works at a lathe in the shop, at a desk in the office, at a table in the laboratory, or at a counter in the store, he is God's priest in that place, and whatever he says or does must reflect the glory of God.

It is very difficult for one who works on an assembly line to see how the affixing of three nuts to their respective bolts can have any regal or priestly significance, but this is because we are not trained to see how God uses *things* to open up doors of ministry. Jesus took advantage of a well curb when He was tired to talk to one woman who was a social outcast, and through her ministered to a whole city. So priests of God can use coffee-breaks and lunch hours in our own day of industrialization.

One of the major differences between Judaism and the Christian community is that under the former the important thing was the place where the sacrifice was offered, while under the latter, place has lost significance. The true worshipper no longer thinks in terms of a particular site or city as "the place where men ought to worship" but in terms of spirit and reality.

Under the Levitical priesthood men had to go where the high priest was in order to sacrifice, but our high priest left heaven to come where men were, and by so doing he lifted worship from the drudgery of time and place and made it universal as to both. God can only be confined by what he has made, and never by anything which men have made. "God that made the world and all things therein, seeing that he is Lord of heaven and earth, dwelleth not in temples made with hands, neither is worshipped with men's hands, as though he needed anything."

It is a tremendous challenge which confronts us. We

must undo the crystallizing trend of centuries, and turn back the tide of ecclesiasticism which has engulfed and overwhelmed the ideal of God. We must instil in the hearts of men a recognition of the placelessness of worship and the universality of priesthood of the chosen generation comprising the citizenry of the holy nation. In short, we must restore to earth the dream of the prophets and the vision of the apostles. We must uncover the Word and discover the Way.

PRIESTHOOD AND MINISTRY

The Roman Catholic Church has built up a system of special priesthood on a hierarchical basis, the grounds for which we will examine in subsequent chapters. In approximation to this the Protestant world generally has adopted a clergy system which relegates the members to what is referred to as "lay status," and which effectively negates the new covenant ideal of universal priesthood. Thus the concept of "the priesthood of all believers" has virtually been lost, or if it is still professed it is not given spiritual emphasis in practice.

There are a great many factors which contribute to this. One is the mistaken view concerning the nature of the church, which is no longer regarded as a functioning body served actively by every member, but is looked upon as an institution which may purchase services in its own behalf. A general apathy toward intensive study of the Bible has created a widespread ignorance of the language of revelation and its connotations. Too, the clergy system is now so venerable with age that it is accepted as of divine origin. It is believed that the Christian religion would be powerless without it.

The community of believers in our day suffers from a confusion of tongues. The terms used in the scriptures are often applied to those things which are foreign or alien to their original meaning, and new words have been coined to describe Biblical concepts which serve only to warp or distort them. General terms are given only a specific meaning, and vice versa.

For one to attempt a recapture of the original faith and order as set forth by the holy apostles means that he must recover the meaning attached to the words used by the Spirit. Frequently this means stripping from such words the ecclesiastical ideas with which they have been clothed. When this is done it becomes obvious that the true meaning has been concealed for many generations.

A good illustration of what we mean is found in the words "minister" and "ministry." These appear as translations of Greek terms, but they have been given such limitations in our day that the majesty and breadth originally attached to them has been all but lost.

"Minister" is from the Latin *ministro*, which means "to serve, to attend, to wait on." A minister is one who serves, and any service rendered is ministry. The word "minister" designates one as a servant but never, of itself, expresses or suggests the kind of service rendered. One simply cannot tell by looking at the word the nature of the service. To use the word ministry in such a manner as to apply it exclusively to one branch or field of service is to do an injustice to the language of the Spirit.

In spite of this, to speak of "the minister" in our day is to refer to only one functionary. In justification for this it is urged that Paul declared that he was "made a minister" (Eph. 3: 7), that Tychicus was "a faithful minister in the Lord" (Eph. 6: 21), that Epaphras was "a faithful minister of Christ" (Col. 1: 7), and that Timothy was told how to become "a good minister" (1 Tim. 4: 6). What does this mean? Simply that these men were good servants, faithful in whatever relationship they were called upon to sustain to God, Christ and the congregation.

"Minister" is from *diakonos*, which occurs 30 times. It is rendered minister 20, deacon 3, and servant 7 times. It is translated "deacon" in Philippians 1: 1, 1 Timothy 3: 8, 12. To employ it to designate a special type of labor in a congregation, exclusive of that done by the deacons would be absurd in the light of God's revelation. Yet when one asks a friend to come and hear "the new minister" he is not inviting him to listen to a speech by a newly appointed deacon. Nor does the term "associate minister" refer to an assistant to the deacons. One who decides to "study for the ministry" is not planning to train for the diaconate in most places. Yet the word "deacon" is a transliteration of the Greek word for minister.

The word for minister is found in John 2: 5, 9 where it is applied to the servants who drew water which was then changed into wine by Jesus. It is apparent that one could argue that a minister is "a drawer of water" with as much scriptural ground as he could contend that a minister is "a preacher of the gospel."

Phoebe is called "a minister of the church which is at Cenchrea" (Romans 16: 1) but we would hardly surmise that she was sent forth by the congregation as an evangelist. Those religious bodies which claim to oppose "women ministers" find themselves in difficulty with Phoebe, whom the apostle Paul commended as a minister of a local congregation.

Of course there is nothing in the term "servant" which defines the type of service. The nature of the service is not inherent in the word. The word servant does not mean gardener, chauffeur, maid or cook. There is a difference in saying that "A cook is a servant," and in saying, "A servant is a cook." So there is a great difference between the statements, "A gospel preacher is a minister," and "A minister is a gospel preacher."

A preacher is a minister in the congregation, but so is the custodian who cuts the grass and sweeps the floor, the one who supervises the nursery, and the one who prints and folds the bulletins. Those who use their cars to transport others to the meetings, who visit the homes for the aged, and who look after the needy, are all ministers. It is at this point we have been betrayed into a way of life and speech which contravenes God's plan and purpose. We have actually squeezed the words of the Holy Spirit until we have wrung them dry of their content.

Only one man's name appears upon the signboard with the caption—Minister. The same name appears upon the letterheads and stationery, and upon the bulletins and mailing pieces. By the very designation of one as *the* minister, we have successfully convinced all of the others that they are not ministers. They do not even think of themselves in that category.

If you address a group of members in the foyer with the question, "Are you gentlemen ministers of the congregation," the laughing reply will be, "No, the minister is in the office." Even more ridiculous in the light of the scriptures is for one to reply, "I am not a *minister,* I am just a *deacon.*" This is the equivalent of saying, "I am not a minister, I am just a minister." It is little wonder that the church is confused.

A further indication of our "confusion of tongues" is demonstrated when we talk of one "preparing to enter the ministry." We mean by it that the person under consideration expects to make a professional career out of preaching the gospel. It is only fair to state, however, that he will be expected to take courses designated as homiletics, hermeneutics, pastoral psychology, church administration, religious communications, etc. All of this would have been wholly unintelligible to the apostles and to the communities of saints planted by their labors.

"Ministry," "ministering," and "ministration," come from *diakonia*, which is used 34 times in the new covenant scriptures. It first occurs in Luke 10: 40 where Martha was said to be "distracted with much serving." One might infer from this that a student who went to college to prepare for the ministry would major in "home economics," with a minor in "table settings." Martha was so deeply involved in ministering that she made application to Jesus for an "assistant minister." "Lord, do you not care that my sister has left me to serve (minister) alone? Tell her to help me."

The word for ministry and ministering is employed for the daily distribution of food (Acts 6: 1), for the administration of funds to the famine-ridden and drought-stricken Judean saints (2 Cor. 8: 4, 9: 1), for the work of Paul (2 Cor. 11: 8), and that of Timothy (2 Tim. 4: 5). Thus a person is engaged in ministry whether he is serving tables, carrying funds to the unfortunate, proclaiming the truth, or in any other fashion serving others.

There is nothing distinctive in the word "ministry" as to the kind of service performed. There are two great sources of intellectual evil in the interpretation of God's revelation. One is to create distinctions where God has made none; the other is to destroy or lose sight of the distinctions which God has made.

It is not too much to say that the life of the saint is expressed in the word ministry, or service. Jesus came not to be ministered unto, but to minister. He declared that he was among men as one who served. Those who follow him must come to minister, and not to be ministered unto. The community of believers should have as a goal the providing of an opportunity for every member to share in constructive fashion his thinking and gifts. Any system which commits the edification of the body to one person hired for the role, and reduces the rest to mere spectators is contrary to the plan and purpose of God.

It is at this point that the modern institutional church, while professing to be God's agency for transformation of the world, actually operates to defeat the divine intention. The church envisions itself as a rival of other religious institutions. It is concerned with its "image" in society. It therefore becomes involved in presenting good programs to impress the visiting public, which it calls "worship services," but which consist chiefly of ritualistic or liturgical performances.

There is no question but what the gatherings of the saints in apostolic times were in the nature of family reunions. The spontaneity and unrehearsed participation was of the type which you might expect to find in our day when a Christian family sits down at the Thanksgiving table. Even the least one is heard with special appreciation, and those who are less forward are gently urged to share in the occasion.

Since religion has become highly organized by promoters, whose motivations may be quite genuine and sincere, it has had to invent and devise new offices and officers to keep it moving with accelerated pace. The idea of a personal heart-to-heart relationship with God through the Spirit has been replaced with the philosophy that one should be allied with "a successful church." Such a church is one that enjoys good social relationships and attracts the right people whose presence can lend it an aura of respectability.

It is for this reason that the more dire need there is in a community the farther the church removes itself from it. The desperately poor do not help the image of the church by being within it. Instead they serve only to salve the consciences of the membership by allowing them to make contributions to relieve those whom they never expect to personally encounter.

The "local minister" is the front man for the congregation in our day. He is the key to its popularity or its waning influence. Often a great deal of investigation is made before negotiations begin for his hiring. His personal mannerisms, dress, tone quality and pulpit aplomb come under close scrutiny. A great deal of behind-the-scenes arguing may go on as to the relative merits of several candidates for the post. If a majority of the members of the committee are from one school, an alumnus from that subsidiary institution stands a better chance than one from another alma mater.

So much is this a part of the institutional religious life of our day that it comes with a shock of surprise when one points out that it is utterly foreign to the concept enunciated by the holy apostles. The "local minister" or "one-man pastor" is unknown to the new covenant scriptures. The community of the saints was edified and strengthened by the use of every gift. The believers never gathered to hear a "sermon." The word is not even found in the sacred scriptures. Origen was called "the father of the sermon."

The royal priesthood has certain rights which are divinely given. These rights are accompanied by the responsibility to use them. They cannot be abrogated or transferred without doing serious injury to the body, or despite to the Spirit of grace. One of the basic rights is that of every faithful child of God who has the ability, to speak to his fellows for their edification and comfort. In the primitive congregations men were urged to seek this above all other spiritual gifts.

Of course this meant that the public expression of worship was so arranged as to provide for this exercise, since it would be ridiculous to urge all to seek the ability to edify and then relegate the function to one imported for a fee. Instead of one taking all of the time, the brethren were taught to yield the speaking privilege to one another in love (1 Corinthians 14: 30, 31). And to this fact the scholarship of the world gives ready agreement. Read carefully the following statements from eminent historians.

"The participation in worship was not confined to the official members, but to every male member it was permitted to utter his apprehension of truth. The ordinary services of the church were very similar to those of a good prayer meeting at the present time." (A. H. Newman, D.D., LL.D., *Manual of Church History,* page 141).

"The form of worship of the primitive church was also exceedingly simple. Meetings were held commonly on the first day of the week in private houses or in some public building appropriated to that purpose. At those meetings prayer was offered, portions of the Old Testament and letters from the apostles were read, psalms and perhaps hymns were sung; and words 'of exhortation' were spoken freely by anyone who might feel moved to do this." (Andrew C. Zenas, Professor of Biblical Theology, McCormick Theological Seminary, *Compendium of Church History,* page 28).

"The major premise of every true conclusion as to the ministry of the Apostolic Age, must be the outpouring of the Spirit, hailed by Peter at Pentecost as the mark of Messianic times. In it Moses' ideal that all the Lord's people should be prophets was in substance fulfilled. Accordingly in their worship, as we see from 1 Corinthians 14, each believer was free to edify his fellows by psalm, teaching, revelation, tongue, interpretation, as well as prayer or Eucharist. Whatever limitations expediency came in time to impose on this diffused ministry, the idea involved had, and has, abiding force; and it was not the idea underlying the later distinctions between 'clergy' and 'laity.'" (James Vernon Bartlet, M. A., *Ten Epochs of Church History,* page 477).

"Worship in the apostolic age was a spontaneous expression of devout feeling. The order of worship was a free copy of the synagogue service. Selections from the Old Testament were read. Expositions of Scripture and spontaneous speaking followed." (George P. Fisher, *History of the Christian Church,* page 141).

"The meeting described by the apostle (1 Corinthians 14) is not to be taken as something which might be seen only in Corinth but was peculiar to that city; it may be taken as a type of the Christian meeting throughout the Gentile Christian churches; for the apostle, in his suggestions and criticisms continually speaks of what took place throughout all the churches. What cannot fail to strike us in this picture is the untrammeled liberty of the worship, the possibility of every male member of the congregation taking part in the prayers and exhortations, and the consequent responsibility laid on the whole community to see that the service was for edification." (Thomas M. Lindsay, D.D., Principal of Glasgow College of the United Free Church of Scotland, *The Church and the Ministry in the Early Centuries,* page 48).

"That two or three should thus take part, and all being 'done unto edifying', was, and still should be, a matter for dependence upon, and leading by, the Holy Spirit. No uncontrolled impulse is to be allowed. Gradually, however, clerical power became dominant, and the worship and testimony of a local church was committed to the control of one man, who became known as 'the minister'. This was an easy way of seeking to regulate difficulties, but it was not God's way. Two wrongs do not make a right. The system of 'the one-man ministry' spread over Christendom and remained general, until many of God's people were awakened to the importance of adhering to New Testament principles and recognizing the prerogatives and claims of the Holy Spirit in the gatherings of a church; they realized the unscripturality of the stifling of the development of spiritual gifts by the appointment of one man to conduct the services. The Lord will have regard in the coming Day of reward to those who, amidst disrepute and criticism, have sought to remain faithful to Him and obedient to His will as revealed in God's Word." (W. E. Vine, M.A., *First Corinthians,* page 196).

"We understand edification here in its general and original sense, as given to it in St. Paul's writings, as referring to the advancement and development, from its common ground, of the whole church. The edification, in this sense, was the common work of all. Even edification by the Word was not assigned exclusively to one individual; every man who felt the inward call to it might give utterance to the Word in the assembled church." (Dr. Augustus Neander, Ordinary Professor of Theology in the University of Berlin, *Church History,* Vol. 1, page 251).

"From this (1 Corinthians 14: 26) and other passages it is clear that the upbuilding of the church was not confined then, as now, to one, or at most two, of the congregation; but was the privilege of all the members, and though such a practice is liable to abuse (James 3: 1), it is possible that its entire disuse has led to still greater evils obvious to all—'quenching of the Spirit.'" (Robert Young, author of Young's Analytical Concordance).

"There is no doubt, that in the ordinary Lord's Day meeting of the apostolic churches, quite a number of brethren took part in the speaking and praying. This is clear to any one who will read carefully the fourteenth chapter of First Corinthians. It is true that the instructions contained in that chapter are mostly given to persons possessed of spiritual gifts; but if, when men possessed of such gifts were in the church, it was not best that any one of them should occupy the entire time, why should we think it best to reverse the rule in the absence of such gifts? Surely we have no right to make such a change unless there be something in the absence of spiritual gifts which demands it." (J. W. McGarvey, *Apostolic Times,* 1873).

Since it cannot be denied that in the days of the apostles the edification of the congregations was not limited to one or two men, but was the privilege of all who were faithful and able, and that this precedent was by actual disposition of the Holy Spirit, and with apostolic approval and regulation, it remains for us to enquire upon what grounds the principle is now ignored and a wholly different system inaugurated which was unknown to the early saints?

The most common excuse for the modern substitution is that the picture given in the New Testament belongs to the days of spiritual gifts bestowed by the laying on of apostolic hands, and consequently is not binding upon the church today in the absence of such gifts. But was not every letter written to and regulating the churches, penned in the days of spiritual gifts? Then by what reasoning can we apply any of the new covenant letters to the congregations in our day? If we can carelessly dismiss the plan of edification authorized "when the whole congregation assembles," can we not dismiss all other instructions given to the believers?

If the system of hiring one man to speak to the assembled congregation each time is superior to that of having "all speak one by one" (1 Corinthians 14: 31), why did not the Holy Spirit bestow the gift to edify only upon the most talented one in each congregation?

It is not denied that men possess natural gifts and abilities in these days. Supernatural gifts belong to the supernatural era of the Christian dispensation and natural gifts belong to the natural era. Will not the very same principles which governed the use of supernatural gifts to the edification of the assembly also govern the use of the natural gifts to the same end?

The Holy Spirit uses the term *charisma* to designate the gifts. Concerning this word and its usage we insert herewith a statement from Fenton John Anthony Hort, D.D., Lady Margaret's Reader in Divinity, University of Cambridge, in his well-known work, *The Christian Ecclesia,* page two:

"Charisma comes of course from charizomai; it means anything given of free bounty not of debt, contract or right. It is thus obviously used in Philo, and as obviously in Romans 5: 15; 6: 23; and less obviously, but I believe the same force in the other passages of St. Paul, as also in the only other New Testament place, 1 Peter 4: 10. In these instances it is used to designate what we call 'natural advantages' independent of any human process of acquisition, or advantage freshly received in the course of Providence; both alike being regarded as so many free gifts from the Lord to men, and as designed by Him to be distinctive qualifications for rendering distinctive service to men, or communities of men."

Inasmuch as the Holy Spirit employed the identical term to designate both natural and supernatural gifts, referring to the gift of sexual control (1 Corinthians 7: 7) in exactly the same fashion as the direct manifestations of 1 Corinthians 12: 4, can we not conclude that all gifts or abilities are to be utilized for "the common good" (1 Corinthians 12: 7), regardless of the method of bestowal? And would not a system which makes impossible the functioning of the abilities of all the brethren today be as obnoxious to God as the same system would have been in Corinth in the days of Paul?

The Holy Spirit moved Peter to write to the exiles of the Dispersion, "As each has received a gift, employ it for one another, as good stewards of God's grace" (1 Peter 4: 10). Would the same Spirit, if writing to us today, change the message to read, "Let each stifle his natural gifts, and employ another, as a good steward of God's grace"?

If the apostle Paul wrote to a congregation in Rome in the twentieth century, would he say, "I myself am satisfied about you, my brethren, that you yourselves are full of goodness, filled with all knowledge and able to instruct one another" (Romans 15: 14), or would he recommend that they hire a "local minister"? Inasmuch as he was satisfied with them, and about them, would he be satisfied with our modern substitution which, while the people love to have it so, makes impossible the functioning of the assembly as Paul outlined it?

When the apostle addressed his first letter to the congregation at Thessalonica, he emphasized the fact of the coming of our Lord, adding, "Therefore encourage one another and build one another up, just as you are doing" (1 Thessalonians 5: 11). Is there a better time to exercise the members in building one another up than when all have gathered in one place. This was God's program for the congregation originally. Has he altered it for the present time? Who will affirm that an uninspired man may utilize all of the time appointed for public edification, when an inspired man was not permitted to do so?

The system into which the religious world has fallen has created the greatest "brain drain" in history. It is directly responsible for accumulation of a tremendous mass of unused talent. In many congregations there are brilliant men who are never allowed to share their thinking with the rest of the saints and faithful brethren simply because they are not regarded as being in the clerical caste.

Superintendents of schools, college professors, attorneys, advertising executives, and many others, are doomed to a life of perpetual silence in the public meetings by this system. Men who are invited to address conventions of learned personnel are never invited to share their thinking in the public assembly of the congregations where they attend. Often they are forced to listen to one who invades their professional field in his remarks, although quite ignorant of the subject upon which he professes to speak with authority.

Congregations need to hear the personal testimony of men who are in daily contact with life as it is being lived. Those who teach science in the college classroom are more qualified to speak about the problems raised by modern research than one who never studied the subject. The psychiatrist in the congregation should be more capable of talking about emotional and personality disorders than one whose observation is limited and who has no technical knowledge of the subject.

Why should a congregation not be allowed to share in all of the helpful insights of all of its membership? Why muzzle men who are often more scholarly and qualified than the one who is hired to project the orthodox position week after week? That many are growing weary with the sterility which has resulted is obvious. A reaction is setting in which takes the form of a revolution. In many areas "an underground church" is forming.

This phenomenon is observable when people become tired of meaningless and monotonous ritual, of forms and ceremonies. Small groups begin to meet in homes without benefit of clergy, and in these cell meetings all are free to speak their honest sentiments and convictions. No one lords it over the others. There is no clergy-laity division. It is apparent that many are hungering and thirsting after righteousness and want to feed themselves.

The royal priesthood should be made to realize that divine rights have been surrendered to, or captured by, a special caste, an incipient clergy. These rights must be returned to the saints, or God's plan of the ages will be nullified as it pertains to our responsibility. By what scriptural authority do men set themselves up, or offer themselves for hire, as *the ministers* of the congregations?

On what bases do some of the priests claim such exaltation, eminence, enthronement and esteem, over the other regal princes of the priesthood of heaven? Is it by virtue of a more noble birth? Is it the result of superior knowledge conveyed to them by other mortals? Are they composed of a more worthy clay which elevates the fortunate ones thus created to shine as brighter constellations in the Christian galaxy?

Every Christian is a priest! Every Christian is a minister! Every priest of God has a divine right as a minister of God to serve the King of kings and his loyal subjects. Every talent must be utilized in God's service. Every man who has the ability to exhort, edify or comfort his brethren must be granted the right to do so. God has placed no pulpit as a throne in the midst of the congregation, to which one man has an exclusive right.

The freedom of the speaker's platform for every loyal capable subject must be asserted, or we must admit that a part of the worship of God belongs to a stipendiary, and in that phase of devotion we can only approach God through human mediators, financially supported by the saints "to perform their ritual duties." Since this is the function of priests (Hebrews 9: 6) we will then have a special caste of priests above their fellows, and we will take steps toward Rome.

E. De Pressense has written: "We have already shown that the universal priesthood was only maintained to its full extent in practice, as well as in theory, so long as the redemptive sacrifice of Christ was accepted without reserve as the source of universal salvation. He is the one Priest of the Church only if He truly finished all upon the cross, so that His disciples have but to appropriate His sacrifice by faith, in order to become priests and kings in Him and by Him. If all was not completed on Calvary, if the salvation of man is not a perfected work, then we are still separated from God; we have no free access into his sanctuary, and we seek mediators who may present our offering for us. When Christianity is regarded rather as a new law than as the sovereign manifestation of Divine grace, it leaves us in our impotence, our unworthiness, to our fruitless strivings and our partial aspirations. We are no more kings and priests, we fall back under the yoke of a servile fear. The hierarchy gains by all that men lose of childlike confidence in that infinite mercy which alone renders needless all official mediation between the penitent and God." (*The Early Years of Christianity,* Volume 4, pages 47, 48. Translated by Annie Harwood-Holmden).

THE CASE FOR A SPECIAL PRIESTHOOD

Fairness demands that we consider and examine the position of those who uphold the idea of a special priesthood, and who seek to establish a difference among God's people represented by the terms "clergy" and "laity." Since this doctrine seems to reach its ultimate in the Roman Catholic Church, we will carefully scrutinize the position of that great religio-politico institution on the issue. Before me lies the booklet by Rev. John A. O'Brien, Ph.D., entitled *"The Priesthood: A Divine Institution."* It has a sub-heading: "The Priest is Christ's Ambassador to Men." The booklet bears the approval signatures of Very Rev. Msgr. T. E. Dillon as Censor Librorum; and John Francis Noll, D.D., Bishop of Fort Wayne. Surely if it is possible to make out a logical case for the special priesthood this booklet should be able to accomplish it, since it was written for that very purpose.

In our examination of its postulates and alleged proofs, we shall present it *in toto,* lest we be accused of scrapping the arguments or omitting something vital to the conclusion. Our method will be to print it section by section and test its claims as we proceed. In some cases we will notice and comment upon each sentence, in others we shall deal with a whole paragraph; this dependent upon the nature of the argument involved. Below is the introductory section of the booklet.

> **The Catholic Church differs from the various denominations in that it alone possesses an altar and a priesthood. It worships Almighty God not alone by prayer but by sacrifice as well. It offers up in an unbloody manner the Sacrifice of Christ on Calvary. This sacrifice was foreshadowed in the Old Law by the bloody sacrifice of the priesthood of Levi, the offerings of sheep and goats and oxen. The offering of the sacrifice of bread and wine by Melchisedech, King of Salem, and priest of the Most High, typified the clean oblation of which the prophet Malachi spoke: "From the rising of the sun even unto the going down of the same my name is great among the Gentiles, and in every place there is sacrifice and there is offered to my name a clean oblation, saith the Lord of hosts." Such is the divinely inspired prophecy concerning that clean oblation, the holy Sacrifice of the Mass which constitutes the central act of worship in the Church founded by Christ.**
>
> **Without a priesthood, however, there can be no altar and no sacrifice, as the experience of our separated brethren abundantly demonstrates. There can be preaching and prayer. But that essential element of worship, sacrifice, which bulks so large in the Old Testament, is lost without a priesthood. Did Christ found a Church but make no provision for a priesthood to offer sacrifice? Did He fail to institute a priesthood which would continue in all ages the work He had begun? Did He launch His bark without captain or crew to guide it over the uncharted waters of the centuries yet to come?**

We have no more desire to defend the various denominations than we do the Roman Church, for neither constitute the New Testament congregation of saints established by our Lord through His holy apostles. The churches of Christ have a priesthood. It is composed of all those who are God's own people (1 Peter 2: 9) and these priests worship God not only by prayer but by "spiritual sacrifices acceptable to God through Jesus Christ" (1 Peter 2: 5).

The Romish priesthood which "offers up in an unbloody manner the Sacrifice of Christ on Calvary" is doing that which no child of God was ever authorized to do, and while it is true that the real sacrifice of our Lord was prefigured and adumbrated by the offering of sheep and goats and oxen, "when Christ appeared as a high priest of the good things that have come, then through the greater and more perfect tent, he entered *once for all* into the Holy Place, taking not the blood of goats and calves but his own blood, thus securing an eternal redemption" (Heb. 9: 11, 12). Since the mass is supposed to be a daily offering in an unbloody manner of the sacrifice of Christ on the cross, the Romish priests like those of Judaism "go continually—performing their ritual duties" (Heb. 9: 6). But of Christ it is affirmed that he need "not offer himself repeatedly" but "has appeared once for all at the end of the age to put away sin by the sacrifice of himself" (Heb. 10: 25, 26). The Roman Catholic Church is an unholy mixture of Jewish ritualism, pagan superstition, and Christian revelation.

Melchizedek did not offer a sacrifice of bread and wine. He merely brought forth common items of sustenance, and with them refreshed Abraham and his servants on their return from battle. Josephus says: "Now this Melchizedek supplied Abram's army in an hospitable manner, and *gave them provisions in abundance, and as they were feasting,* he began to praise him, and to bless God for subduing his enemies under him" (Antiquities of Jews 1-10-2). Melchizedek no more intended to offer a sacrifice than did Abraham, who when confronted by visitors said, "Rest yourselves under the tree, while I fetch a morsel of bread, that you may refresh yourselves" (Gen. 18: 4, 5).

In order to justify this disorted interpretation the Douay Version has rendered Genesis 14: 18, "But Melchisedech the king of Salem, bringing forth bread and wine, *for* he was the priest of the most high God." But the Romanist translators do not hesitate to translate the same Hebrew word which they render "for" by the word "and" in other places.

We are indebted to the Hebrew letter for virtually all that we know of the nature and character of Melchizedek and his priesthood. Since that letter was written to prove that the order of Melchizedek was superior to that of Levi, and the subject was priesthood, it would have bolstered the argument immensely to have established that Melchizedek offered a sacrifice of bread and wine in type of the Lord's death on Calvary, and the memorial which he ordained of that event. However, when the apostle records the connection of Melchizedek with the father of the Jews, he merely says that he "met Abraham returning from the slaughter of the kings and blessed him" (Heb. 7: 1). There is no hint in the Holy Scriptures that he offered a sacrifice of bread and wine, so we must put this down as a figment of imagination conjured up to support a questionable practice.

The words of Malachi (1: 11) are said to be "a divinely inspired prophesy concerning that clean oblation, the holy Sacrifice of the Mass." But the mass is nowhere mentioned in the New Covenant writings which constitute our only source of information relative to the fulfillment of prophecy concerning the kind of sacrifices which God will honor. In Peter 2: 5 it is distinctly said that God's holy priesthood will offer up *spiritual sacrifices* acceptable to God. Accordingly every child of God is required to present his body "a living sacrifice" (Rom. 12: 1). In the Hebrew letter, which more than any other deals with sacrifice, we are urged, "Through him then let us continually offer up a sacrifice of praise to God, that is the fruit of lips that acknowledge his name" (13: 15). In Malachi 1: 11 the expression "my name" is used by the Lord three times, and the reason assigned for incense and a pure offering in every place is "for my name shall be great among the heathen, said the Lord of hosts." Is it not logical to believe that the fruit of lips that acknowledge his name constitute the offering and incense to which Malachi makes reference?

To this argument the Romanists file two objections. They demand to know how the fruit of our lips in hallowed praise can be an antitype of incense and sacrifice. We reply with the words of David, "Let my prayer be counted as incense, before thee, and the lifting up of my hands as an evening sacrifice" (Psa. 141: 2). In the vision which John beheld he saw "golden bowls full of incense, which are the prayers of the saints" (Rev. 5: 8). We conclude then that these represent a fulfillment of the prophecy of Malachi, and that there is no room here for arbitrarily asserting that the ancient prophet was speaking of the mass.

The second objection to our interpretation is that the word "*mincha*" translated "offering" in the passage by Malachi, always means literal sacrifice and cannot be applied to a figurative or spiritual sacrifice. This objection is invalid as evidenced in Isaiah 66: 20, where *mincha* twice occurs in one verse, and the first time must be employed in a figurative sense. "And they shall bring all your brethren from the nations *as an offering* to the Lord . . . just as the Israelites bring their cereal *offering* in a clean vessel to the house of the Lord."

We have demonstrated that in the New Testament plan there is a priesthood and there are sacrifices. As to the altar, the apostle affirms "We have an altar from which those who serve the tent have no right to eat" (Heb. 13: 10). So Christ did not "found a church and make no provision for a priesthood to offer sacrifice." He did not "fail to institute a priesthood which would continue in all ages the work He had begun." He did not "launch His bark without captain or crew to guide it over the uncharted waters of the centuries yet to come." He is the captain of our salvation (Hebrews 2: 10) and every member of the church is part of that crew. Every member is a priest and a minister. What Rome must do to substantiate her claim is to show that God ordained a captain, a crew, and a third class composed of *paying passengers* who are on board not to serve, but to be served. It is here at the first attempt that Dr. O'Brien's thesis on a special priesthood breaks down, and his argument like an ill-manned vessel is left floundering. Let us notice his next argument.

A STRANGE PROCEDURE

That Christ acted in this strange manner would seem to be the belief of our Protestant friends. For in their eyes the minister who preaches to them is clothed with no divine power. His authority comes solely from the congregation which employs him. He is like the artist who plays the organ, the secretary who keeps the books, and like them is dismissable at the will and caprice of the congregation which hires him.

That Christ did not act in the strange manner above described, founding a Church but failing to make any provision for its perpetuation through a definite ministry, has been the constant belief of the Church which He founded. The Church teaches that Christ not only instituted the priesthood but conferred upon it clearly specified powers and authority. It is inconceivable to her that a divine Being, Jesus

Christ, would found a Church to minister to the spiritual needs of mankind in the succeeding ages without establishing a ministry and conferring upon it the power and authority necessary to enable the church to fulfill her divinely appointed mission. Such is the procedure which both reason and common sense would lead us to expect.

Such is the procedure which the New Testament shows us Christ *actually* followed. It tells us that Christ selected twelve Apostles and ordained them His first priests. Upon them He conferred the power of ordaining others to continue their work. The sacrament by which men are ordained and receive the Power and grace to discharge the duties of the priestly office is Holy Orders.

It is apparently inconceivable to the priestly writer that a church may exist without a special priesthood claiming dogmatic authority or a hired minister subject to the whims of his employers. Yet, strange to say, no New Testament congregation ever hired a man as the minister to preach to them. Such a thing as hiring and firing the minister was as unknown to the primitive churches, as playing an organ in the public worship expressions of the church. The scribe is more nearly correct than he realized, when he states of the hired minister, "He is like the artist who plays the organ." That is true, for neither the hired minister nor the organ player is found in the scriptural description of the church which was purchased by the blood of our Lord.

Christ did not found a church and fail to provide for its perpetuation through a definite ministry, but that definite ministry is composed of all of the saints. True, there are bishops over each local congregation of disciples to shepherd them, and deacons in each local congregation to attend to the care of the needy ones, but these are chosen from among the membership by the whole multitude of believers, and there is no higher position of authority than to be one of several bishops of a local congregation. A plurality of bishops over one church is clearly taught in the Sacred Scriptures; one bishop over a plurality of churches is not taught therein.

The writer makes two expressions synonymous. They are "instituting a priesthood" and "establishing a ministry." Jesus Christ did this very thing, but the ministry and priesthood he established are universal as related to Christians, and not confined to a sacerdotal group as Rome would have it. It is observable that the author says, "*The Church* teaches that Christ not only instituted the priesthood but conferred upon it clearly specified powers and authority." We do not have time, space nor inclination at this point to argue the right of "the church" to teach, but suffice it to say, we have definite logical grounds for respecting the revelation of God as the only authoritative teaching on matters of religious interest. We shall demand and expect a "Thus saith the Lord" as a proper criterion for judging the worthiness of any doctrine affecting our spiritual welfare.

Dr. O'Brien affirms that the procedure which he defends is shown by the New Testament to be the one which Christ actually followed. It is here the battle can be properly joined. It is true that Christ selected twelve apostles, but it is not true that he "ordained them His *priests*" in a special sense. That they were special ambassadors of the absent King, the Bible teaches (2 Cor. 5: 29), but that they were high priests, or even *higher* priests, than the remainder of the saints, is not true. They became priests of God, not by ordination, but by acceptance of our Lord and obedience to His commands. This is true of every child of God.

The apostle upon whom Rome relies the most is Peter. It seems as if the Holy Spirit, in view of the unprincipled use to be made of this apostle by a modern priestcraft, selected him to be the one to declare in unmistakable language the great doctrine of the priesthood of all believers. Peter shows that everyone who comes to the "living stone rejected by men" becomes in turn "a living stone" built into a holy priesthood. Thus to become a priest is conditioned only upon coming to Christ (1 Peter 2: 5). God's priests are those who are "chosen and destined by God the Father and sanctified by the Spirit for obedience to Jesus Christ and for sprinkling with his blood" (1 Peter 1: 2). The apostles shared "the priesthood" with every other citizen of heaven's rule, for that realm is "a kingdom of priests."

Rome not only demands a belief in "seven sacraments" but even in the ritualistic forms attendant upon the administration of them. "I also profess, that there are truly and properly seven sacraments of the new law, instituted by Jesus Christ, our Lord, and necessary for the salvation of mankind, though not all for everyone: To wit, Baptism, Confirmation, Eucharist, Penance, Extreme Unction, Orders and Matrimony, and that they confer grace; and that of these, Baptism, Confirmation, and Orders, cannot be reiterated without sacrilege. And I also receive and admit the received and approved ceremonies of the Catholic Church, used in the solemn administration of all the aforesaid sacraments" (*Ordo-Administrandi Sacramenti*, page 65).

The Lord Jesus Christ did not institute confirmation, penance, extreme unction, matrimony, or holy orders. Matrimony was ordained in the primeval garden when God ordained that a man should leave father and mother and cleave unto his wife. This was four thousand years prior to the advent of Christ into the world. Although Christ ordained or appointed the apostles and the seventy, he instituted no formal ceremony of outward ritual. Even great Roman Catholic historians have been forced to admit that "ordination is not truly and properly a Sacrament."

DID THE APOSTLES HAVE "PRIESTLY POWERS"?

The apostate church, in order to establish the claim of the hierarchy, seeks to prove that the apostles were granted three "priestly powers." Reasoning from their assumption that the modern priests are successors to the apostles, they then claim for them these special powers. We shall examine these claims as given in the booklet *"The Priesthood: A Divine Institution."*

THE FIRST ORDINATION

It was instituted by Christ at the Last Supper, when after consecrating the elements of bread and wine ino the Holy Eucharist, He said to the Apostles: "Do ye this for a commemoration of me." (Luke 22: 19) The Council of Trent declares: "If anyone says that by these words: 'Do ye this for a commemoration of me,' that Christ did not constitute the Apostles priests, or did not ordain that they and other priests offer His body and blood, let him be anathema."

At the Last Supper, Jesus Christ, the High Priest of the New Law according to the order of Melchisedech, fulfilled the promise which He had previously made to the Apostles, that He would give them His flesh to eat and His blood to drink. He instituted as a permanent and official act of worship the Eucharistic Sacrifice which He had just offered. In commanding the Apostles to do what He had just done, He gave them the power which that act entails, namely, the power to consecrate. In authorizing them to offer the

self-same Sacrifice which He had instituted, Christ made the Apostles and their successors the sharers of His eternal priesthood.

By the expression "consecrating the elements of bread and wine into the Holy Eucharist" the writer means according to the doctrine of transubstantiation that the bread and wine were changed into the literal body and blood of Christ. The Council of Trent, to which reference is made, says, "Canon I.—If any one shall deny that the body and blood together with the soul and divinity of our Lord Jesus Christ, and therefore entire Christ, are truly, really, and substantially contained in the sacrament of the most holy Eucharist; and shall say that He is only in it as in a sign, or in a figure, or virtually—let him be accursed."

I deny that the bread and fruit of the vine were the literal flesh and blood of our Lord, when he instituted the memorial, for the simple reason that he was standing there in the flesh, and with the blood still in His body, when he gave the elements to the apostles. Since "blood is the life of the flesh," then if the elements were actually His body and blood, there were two Christs present at the final Supper—one a literal, living Christ, the other a dead Christ. But an anathema is pronounced upon one who denies that the soul of Christ is not actually in "the Eucharist." If "the soul and divinity of Christ" were "truly and really contained in the sacraments" they could not at the same time be truly and really contained in his body standing before the apostles. But a body is dead when the soul is not in it, therefore the living Christ would have had to be dead, and the dead Christ would have had to be living.

But both Jesus and the apostles refer to the elements in the same fashion after "consecration" as before. In Matthew 26: 27, 29, "He took a cup, and when he had given thanks he gave it to them saying, 'Drink of it, all of you' . . . I tell you I shall not drink again of this *fruit of the vine* until that day when I drink it new with you in my Father's kingdom." Paul declared that he received of the Lord the information he delivered to the Corinthian congregation relative to the Lord's Supper. He declared that Jesus took bread, gave thanks, broke it and said, "This is my body which is for you." Yet in 1 Corinthians 11: 26, 27, 28 the apostle shows that what was eaten was still bread and not flesh.

The Council of Trent is cited as authority for the idea that by the expression "Do ye this for a commemoration of me," Christ constituted the apostles priests to offer His body and blood. We reject the resolution of this council as having no authority whatsoever. Since the work of the Council of Trent was not concluded until 1563, when its decrees were ratified by Pope Pius IV, that council came 1500 years too late to carry any weight with the true children of God.

But do the words of Christ imply that he was commissioning a special priesthood to offer an unbloody sacrifice? Far from it. The Lord's Supper is a feast, not a sacrifice; it is observed at a table, not an altar; it is eaten, not offered up; it is a communion of a congregation of priests, not an oblation of priests for a congregation. Jesus did not tell the apostles when he ordained the feast "I appoint unto you an altar at which you may officiate," but he did say at that time "As my Father hath appointed a kingdom for me, so do I appoint for you that you may *eat and drink at my table in my kingdom*" (Luke 22: 30). The apostle Paul in connection with the teaching about the Lord's Supper, declares, "You cannot drink the cup of the Lord and the cup of demons. You cannot *partake of the table of the Lord* and the table of demons" (1 Cor. 10: 21). We conclude then that the expression "Do this in remembrance of me" does not refer to official authority to sacrifice at an altar, but to the partaking at a festival board of those emblems of our Lord's sacrifice *once for all.* As proof of this interpretation of the words of our Lord, we cite the fact that Paul delivers the same charge to the whole congregation, and explains them by saying, "For as often as ye eat this bread and drink the cup, you proclaim the Lord's death until he comes" (1 Cor. 11: 26). Thus our Lord meant that we should all eat and drink in memory of Him, and that is all He meant. It is here that the decretals of the Council of Trent and the whole philosophy of Romish priestcraft come tumbling down.

Dr. O'Brien, following the regular line of argument used by the Romanists through the years declares that at the last supper, Jesus fulfilled the prior promise to the apostles that He would give them His flesh to eat and His blood to drink. This is a direct reference to the teaching of our Lord as recorded in John, chapter six, and which the Catholic Church makes applicable to "the Eucharist."

Jesus said, "Truly, truly, I say to you, unless you eat the flesh of the Son of man and drink his blood, you have no life in you; he who eats my flesh and drinks my blood has eternal life, and I will raise him up at the last day. For my flesh is food indeed, and my blood is drink indeed. He who eats my flesh and drinks my blood abides in me, and I in him" (John 6: 52-56). Our Lord did not here refer to the commemorative supper as we shall demonstrate.

It will be agreed by all that the language employed must be accepted as literal or figurative. The Catholic position is that it is literal in import. If this be true, no Catholics except the priests have life, for Jesus said, "Unless you eat the flesh of the Son of man *and drink of his blood,* you have no life in you," and the common members are not allowed to drink the cup. Their reply is that the blood is in the wafer, but if it is, they cannot drink it, for when they have finished the *act of eating* there is nothing left of the wafer. And if the blood of Christ is in the wafer, why does the priest drink the cup? Jesus affirms that he who eats his flesh and drinks his blood has eternal life and will be raised by Him at the last day. If this is to be taken literally, then all who partake of "the Eucharist" will be saved, a thing which Rome denies.

But the context demonstrates that the expression is used figuratively, and has to do with digesting the doctrine and imbibing the spiritual system of teaching, of our Lord. On the previous day, Jesus had fed a multitude of five thousand with two fish and five barley loaves taken from a lad, and the miracle had so affected the people they were about to take Him by force and coronate Him as king. Jesus withdrew, and crossed the sea to Capernaum. The multitude followed Him, expecting to be fed again the next day. Jesus told them that they had sought Him, not because of His power, but because they ate their fill of the loaves. He exhorted them to "not labor for the food which perishes, but for *the food which endures to eternal life,* which the Son of man will give to you."

The hungry mob, still anxious for further food, asked for a miracle such as Moses performed saying "Our fathers ate the manna in the wilderness; as it is written, 'He gave them bread from heaven to eat.'" When Jesus pointed out the bread of God is that which comes down from heaven and gives life to the world, they asked to be fed by such bread always. Then comes a significant statement. Jesus said to them "I am the bread of life; he who *believes in me* shall never thirst"

(John 6: 35). Thus, the hunger is satisfied by *coming to Christ;* the thirst is satisfied by *believing in Christ.* Eating the flesh of the Son of man is equivalent to embracing His tenets; drinking the blood of the Son of man is equivalent to trustful obedience to His will.

That this is a correct view is demonstrated by an occurrence after the lesson delivered in the Capernaum synagogue. Many of his own disciples, not comprehending the spiritual bearing of his message, said "This is a hard saying; who can listen to it?" Jesus said, "Do you take offense at this? . . . It is the spirit that gives life, the flesh is of no avail, *the words that I have spoken unto you are spirit and life*" (John 6: 61-63). Thus, the expression "he who eats my flesh and drinks my blood has eternal life" means simply that he who comes to Christ, and believes on Him, in obedience to His word, is made a partaker of His life, i.e., of His flesh and blood. Again the priestly thesis breaks down.

Our Lord did not institute as a permanent and official act of worship "the Eucharist sacrifice which he had just offered." He instituted a festal table at which every child of God would eat until His return. It is not true that "In commanding the apostles to do what He had just done, He gave them the power to consecration." He merely instructed them to eat and drink in memory of His death. Note too, that all who received the bread, received the cup. Jesus did not at the final supper "authorize them to offer the self-same sacrifice" or any other sacrifice. He ordered them instead to eat and drink at His table—the very opposite of sacrifice. Thus, Rome loses her argument for the first of "three priestly powers." She will lose the others as well.

OTHER PRIESTLY POWERS

Christ completed the communication of His priesthood to the Apostles, when a few days later, he con-

ferred upon them the other strictly sacerdotal power of forgiving sins. On that first Easter Christ appeared to His Apostles and said to them: "As the Father hath sent me, I also send you. When he had said this, he breathed on them: and he said to them: *Receive ye the Holy Ghost. Whose sins you shall forgive, they are forgiven them; and whose sins you shall retain, they are retained.*" (John 20: 21-23)

The Apostles regarded themselves henceforth as ministers of reconciliation. Thus St. Paul writes to the Corinthians: "God hath reconciled us to Himself through Christ, and hath given to us the ministry of reconciliation . . . For Christ, therefore, we are ambassadors; God, as it were exhorting through us." (II Cor. 5: 18-20) In other words God sends Christ to reconcile sinners; Christ sends us. We are His ambassadors of mercy to sinful men, divinely commissioned to cleanse and heal them.

The statement of our Lord is plain, unequivocal and positive. It is undeniable that he gave the apostles the right, privilege or authority to forgive sins. But notice that he did not tell them at the same time how they were to do it. This does not mean we cannot know how they were to accomplish it, for our Lord told them they would receive the Holy Spirit who would guide them unto all things. We need only consult the record of their acts thus to know how they were to forgive and retain sins.

There are but three ways of forgiveness for sins mentioned in the New Testament, as follows: (1) Actual forgiveness; (2) Declared forgiveness; (3) Legislative forgiveness. If we can determine which of these the apostles taught and practiced, after having received the Holy Spirit which was to guide them into all truth, we shall know what our Lord meant when He said, "Whose sins you remit, they shall be remitted."

Did the apostles claim to have the power to *actually* forgive sins? Instead of making such a claim, they taught the very opposite. When Simon attempted to purchase the gift of God with money, Peter said unto him, "Repent therefore of this wickedness of yours and pray to the Lord that, if possible, the intent of your heart may be forgiven you" (Acts 8: 22). If Peter believed in the power of absolution as taught in the Romish "sacrament of penance" he could have demonstrated it here. Instead, he pointed to God as the only one who could actually *forgive* sins. John declared, "If any one does sin, we have an advocate with the Father, Jesus Christ the righteous" (1 John 2: 1). This is far different than saying, "If any man sin we have the sacrament of penance." Rome says that a certain form of absolution is essential and must be pronounced, but nowhere do the apostles make any such allegation. They deny by their practice that Jesus conferred upon them the power to actually forgive sins. This belongs exclusively to God.

Did the apostles exercise a declarative power of forgiveness? That our Lord possessed such power while on earth is quite easily demonstrated. When a certain paralytic was brought to him, he said to the cripple, "Take heart, my son; your sins are forgiven" (Matt. 9: 2). When the scribes who observed this act of mercy said among themselves that Christ was blaspheming, Jesus perceiving their thoughts said, "Which is easier, to say 'Your sins are forgiven,' or to say, 'Rise and walk'? But that you may know that the Son of man has *authority on earth to forgive sins,*" he then said to the paralytic, "Rise, take up your bed and go home." When the crowds saw the man do this, they were afraid, and glorified God who had given such authority to men. Did the apostles have the same authority? Did the statement that they could remit sins, confer the ability to declare such sins remitted as was the case with Christ? If so, the New Testament is absolutely silent about it, and with no testimony on the matter, we can neither affirm nor believe it.

Since there are but three methods of forgiveness revealed in the New Testament, and since the apostles did not employ either of the first two, it is a compelling conclusion that our Savior referred to legislative forgiveness in His statement to them. This means that the apostles were to reveal a law, by compliance with which, the guilty sinner would receive actual forgiveness from God for sins committed. The apostle Paul declares, "The law of the Spirit of life in Christ Jesus has set me free from the law of sin and death" (Rom. 8: 2). From this we learn that we are set free from sin by a law. "You who were once slaves of sin have become obedient from the heart to the standard of teaching to which you were committed, and, having been set free from sin, have become slaves of righteousness" (Rom. 6: 17, 18). Freedom from sin is not obtained by an "absolvo te" pronounced by a priest but by obedience to the standard of teaching.

Rome has much to say about Peter. Let us notice the plan by which this apostle proposed remission of sins to the guilty ones on the day of Pentecost. When they demanded to know what to do, "Peter said to them, 'Repent, and be baptized every one of you in the name of Jesus Christ for the forgiveness of your sins'" (Acts 2: 38). Here is the first announcement of the law by which forgiveness of sins may be secured. It is not by an exercise of sacerdotal authority, but by compliance with the terms specified by the apostle, speaking under the influence of the Spirit.

The priestly advocate quotes 2 Corinthians 5: 18-20, to make it appear that the ministry of reconciliation is manifest in a sacerdotal power to absolve, but a close examination of the previous chapter will disclose that the apostles "having this ministry by the grace of God . . . by the open statement of truth we would commend ourselves to every man's conscience in the sight of God" (2 Cor. 4: 1-3). It is by a statement of the truth, by the proclamation of the terms conveyed by heaven that the sins are remitted. No man possesses the authority to actually or declaratively forgive sins. The second pillar supporting the theory of a special priesthood is thus torn from its moorings. Surely that theory is built upon the sand. Now let us proceed to consideration of the third alleged support.

THIRD GREAT POWER

The third great power which Christ conferred upon His priests is that of preaching the gospel with authority. While this is not so distinctively a sacerdotal power as that of celebrating Mass or of forgiving sins, it is nevertheless a mark of divine delegation which sets them off from the laity. This power of teaching in His name Christ conferred upon His first priests when He said to them: "Going, therefore, teach ye all nations . . . teaching them to observe all things, whatever I have commanded you. And, behold, I am with you all days, even to the consummation of the world" (Matt. 28: 19, 20).

The right of the priests to preach the gospel with authority entails upon the laity the correlative obligation in the following explicit manner: "He that heareth you heareth me; and he that despiseth you despiseth me; and he that despiseth me despiseth him that sent me." (Luke 10: 16)

We have seen that such a "distinctively sacerdotal power as that of celebrating mass or of forgiving sins" was not conferred upon men as Rome teaches, and now we shall learn that "preaching the gospel with authority" is not "a mark of divine legislation which sets them (priests) off from the laity." In a previous chapter we have shown that all of God's people (laity) are a part of the royal priesthood (1 Pet. 2: 9, 10). Instead of divine legislation setting priests apart from the laity, it was divine legislation which made no distinction. God made men and women; Satan made *clergymen*, and clergymen made *laymen!*

It is true that our Lord gave the commission to the apostles to "Go therefore and make disciples of all nations" (Matt. 28: 19). The means of enrolling such students is found in the kindred statement, "Go into all the world and preach the gospel to all creation" (Mark 16: 15). God never commissions a man to do anything without either supernaturally qualifying him to do it, or providing a means by which he may qualify himself naturally to do it. It would be foolish to assume that God would commission a man to do that which was absolutely impossible to accomplish, then condemn him for not doing it. Since the apostles were directly commissioned to teach all nations, it was necessary that they be endued with the ability to speak in the language of every creature. That they were so qualified to be witnesses "unto the end of the earth" (Acts 1: 8) is evident from the fact that on the day of their original proclamation, they "began to speak in other tongues" so that "devout men from every nation under heaven" each heard them speaking in his own language, or native dialect (Acts 2: 4-8). No one can directly operate under "the great commission" today. This commission was given to "witnesses" (Luke 24: 46-48). A witness is one who testifies to facts with which he is conversant. No one today can bear the testimony of these apostles. We can assert our faith in their testimony, and we may re-proclaim that which they testified, but their testimony was as peculiarly their own as their commission to announce it to the world. They fulfilled that commission and accomplished their task, consequently had no successors to their office.

The relationship of the apostles to the church was not personal but *official,* and in this relationship they were to continue to the end of the world. The office of apostles is still in the church, else it has no foundation. All Christians on earth, all members of the household of God are "built upon the foundation of the apostles, and prophets, Christ Jesus himself being the chief cornerstone" (Eph. 2: 20). The apostles are even now in authority, for our Lord said, 'When the Son of man shall sit on his glorious throne, you who have followed me will also sit on twelve thrones, judging the twelve tribes of Israel" (Matt. 19: 28). The apostles occupy the position of authority *in the kingdom of Christ.* "As my Father appointed a kingdom for me, so do I appoint for you that you may eat and drink at my table in my kingdom, and sit on twelve thrones judging the twelve tribes of Israel" (Luke 21: 28).

The commission was not given to the twelve as disciples, but apostles. They fulfilled it by announcing the terms of reconciliation to the entire world, then sealed their testimony with their blood. But there is a difference in the basis of persecution of an ordinary martyr and an apostle. The first dies because he believes what he has heard; the other because he knows what he has seen. Our Lord said to Paul, " I have appeared to you for this purpose, to appoint you to serve and *bear witness to the things which you have seen,* and to those in which I will appear to you" (Acts 26: 16). When the apostles personally completed their work of giving to the world as ambassadors of the Great King, the terms of the treaty in full, the commission was accomplished. They have no successors in office, not simply because no one today can possess the miraculous powers which they needed to confirm their testimony, but because their work of apostleship was completed.

Men now must obtain faith through the testimony of the apostles, just as they did while the apostles were alive. If disputes arise in the congregations we must still "go up to consult the apostles" about the matter. Their revelation is still the criterion by which to measure every act of spiritual significance. Jesus is with them to the end of the age, by maintaining the authority of their teaching, while this world stands. It is true the men are dead but their authoritative teaching remains and we must continue as steadfastly "in the apostles' doctrine" today as on the birthday of the church. When the rich man in Hades besought Abraham to send Lazarus to warn his brothers lest they also come into torment, Abraham said, "They have Moses and the prophets: let them hear them" (Luke 16: 29). Moses and the prophets had been dead for hundreds of years. In what sense did they have them? The reply must be in their authoritative utterances as recorded in the Old Covenant scriptures. In the same sense we have the apostles in their authoritative record of the New Covenant scriptures.

No one is an authoritative proclaimer today as were the apostles. The commission to the apostles is indivisibly connected with miraculous power. After Jesus upbraided the apostles "for their unbelief" (Mark 16: 14) he gave them the commission to "Go into the whole world and preach the gospel to the whole creation." To strengthen them in the tremendous task involved he continues "And these signs will accompany those who believe: in my name they will cast out demons; they will speak in new tongues; they will pick up serpents, and if they drink any deadly thing, it will not hurt them; they will lay hands on the sick; and they will recover." To prove that this was connected with the commission as given, the context shows that "they went forth and preached everywhere, while the Lord worked with them, and confirmed the message by the signs that attended it" (Mark 16: 20). He who operated under authority of the great commission today, should be called upon for his miraculous credentials.

That Rome believes in miracles we do not deny, but that she does not believe that every parish priest possesses power to work miracles is evidenced from the lengthy examination she prosecutes to determine if "miracles" were performed as a prelude to canonization, and the few priests who are designated as saints. Those who claim to be successors to the apostles are convicted as usurpers. Every child of God has a divine right to reproclaim the good news; no one has a right to proclaim it authoritatively. This was reserved for the chosen ambassadors, the holy apostles, and their office has no successors because it was never abdicated. The statement "He that heareth you heareth me; and he that despiseth you despiseth me" was made to the twelve and to them alone. It has no application to a misguided assumptionist who today calls himself "father" in direct antithesis to the teaching of our blessed Lord.

RISE OF THE HIERARCHY

Those who scan the labored attempts of the Roman scholastics to justify their system of priesthood cannot help observing how flimsy is the rational foundation for such a gigantic superstructure. Although affirming that it is based upon God's revelation in the New Covenant scriptures, the defendants must make forced applications of passages wrested from their context, and even then resort to a statement of probabilities. Far from proving that the special priesthood was ordained by Christ and his holy apostles, the chief appeal is to the so-called "fathers," many of whom lived long years this side of the apostles when "the mystery of lawlessness" which already worked in Paul's day, reached its fruition.

"DO YE THIS . . ."

It seems most probable from the evidence afforded by the New Testament that Christ ordained the Apostles priests and empowered them to offer the Eucharistic Sacrifice with no special ceremony but with the simple words: "Do ye this in commemoration of me." Here, as in the case of many of the other sacraments, Christ after instituting the sacrament left it to His Church to determine the matter and form, the precise manner in which the sacrament was to be conferred upon subsequent recipients.

This was apparently determined shortly after the sacrament was instituted. For St. Luke in the Acts of the Apostles and St. Paul in his epistles mention all the elements of the sacrament, namely, the ex-

> **ternal symbolic rite of the imposition of hands and prayer, the internal grace thus communicated, and the institution of the sacrament by Christ. Thus St. Luke writes: "These (the seven deacons) they set before the Apostles, and they praying, imposed hands upon them." (Acts 6: 6) "Then they, fasting and praying, and imposing their hands upon them (Paul and Barnabas) sent them away." (13: 3)**
>
> **Paul and Barnabas ordained priests to carry on their ministry among colonies of newly converted Christians, while the two Apostles moved on to new fields. "And when they had ordained to them priests in every church, they commended them to the Lord, in whom they believed." (14: 22) St. Paul warns Timothy that the sacrament of Orders is to be conferred only on those candidates who give every assurance of fitness for the holy priesthood, saying: "Impose not hands lightly upon any man." (1 Tim. 5: 22).**

The priest, in an attempt to justify his "sacrament of the holy orders" starts with the expression "it seems most probable." But it is neither probable nor possible that Christ ordained the apostles priests in the sense he refers to, for to do so would be to render ineffective the kingdom of priests, composed of all whose sins were washed away by his blood (Rev. 1: 5, 6). We have already learned that the Lord's Supper is a festal observance, participated in by all of God's priests, and not a sacrifice offered by a special priesthood. The congregation was not left to determine "the precise manner in which the sacrament (of orders) was to be conferred," for the word of God knew nothing of any such "sacrament."

In Acts 6: 6, the seven who were selected and appointed as deacons were already "priests of God." Paul and Barnabas were also "priests of God" and were merely given public recognition as having been chosen for a special evangelistic mission, as those who read of their subsequent journey will learn. When they again arrived in Antioch "where they had been commended to the grace of God for *the work which they had fulfilled*" (Acts 14: 26) they gathered the church together and declared all that God had done with them.

Paul and Barnabas did not ordain priests in newly planted congregations. The original word which is mistranslated "priests" by the Roman Catholic version is the Greek "presbuteros" which literally means "an aged person." The word for priest is "hiereus." Nothing can be more palpably misleading than the deliberate translation of a word to justify a practice; thus changing the Bible to suit a human system, rather than changing such a system to suit the Bible. To prove this grave charge I cite the very book of Acts, from which Dr. O'Brien quotes.

There were both "priests" and "elders" among the Jews. Since Rome translates the word "presbuteros" (an aged man) by the term priests in Acts 14: 22, what does she do when the words for both "priests" and "elders" occur in the same verse? Notice the Douay Version at Acts 5: 23: "And being let go, they came to their own company, and related all that the chief priests (archiereis) and ancients (presbuteroi) had said to them." In Acts 23: 14, the Douay Version reads: "Who came to the chief priests (archiereusin) and the ancients (presbuterois)." In Acts 25: 15, "When I was at Jerusalem, the chief priests, and the ancients of the Jews, came unto me." Why did the translators from the Latin Vulgate not render the above by "chief priests *and priests*"? They knew it was obvious that there were both priests and elders among the Jews, and an arbitrary translation of priests for "presbuteros" would be easily detected. Therefore they translated it by the word "ancients," which can be and is used in both an official and non-official sense in the New Covenant scriptures. Why then did they not translate Acts 14: 22 in conformity with their translation elsewhere, to read: "And when they had ordained to them ancients in every church, they commended them to the Lord in whom they believed"? Rome had to get her priestcraft, in, even if she violated all laws of interpretation and forfeited all claims to consistency. Of such fragile, fanciful tissue is the great fabric of priesthood woven.

In 1 Timothy 5: 22, Paul says nothing about "the sacrament of Orders." He is not even dealing with the appointment of men to office. The entire context shows that the subject is discipline of unworthy elders and not appointment of worthy ones. Read 1 Timothy 5: 19-22, where, after Timothy is instructed to admit no charge against an elder, except on evidence of two or three witnesses, he is told to "keep these rules without favor, doing nothing by partiality" and is instructed in connection therewith, "Do not be hasty in the laying on of hands, nor participate in other men's sins," which is but another way of saying, "Do not be hasty in administration of rebuke and discipline and lay yourself liable to a charge of rash judgment; neither be so slow as to be guilty of tolerating and condoning the sins of the guilty." One must not conclude that every time the expression "lay hands on" occurs, that it refers to ordination to office. It certainly does not convey that meaning in Acts 4: 3, where the Jewish rulers came upon Peter and John "and *they laid hands on them,* and put them in prison until the next day."

MERE OFFICEHOLDERS

Some non-Catholic writers have contended that the distinction between clergy and laity arose solely from the need of maintaining good order in the

Church and that the priests were mere officeholders deriving their authority from the congregation. Such a contention is contradicted by the unanimous voice of Christian antiquity. From the earliest days we find express reference in the writings of the Fathers to bishops, priests and deacons, as indeed we do in the Acts of the Apostles and the epistles of St. Paul.

St. Clement is explicit: "Christ is from God, and the Apostles from Christ. Preaching from city to city and throughout the country, the Apostles appointed their first converts, testing them by the Spirit, to be bishops and deacons for the future Christians." (Ad. Cor., 43: 2). He administers a severe rebuke to the Christians of Corinth for daring "to dismiss from the ministry those who had been placed in office by the Apostles or their successors with the approval of the whole Church." (44: 3).

Here is a non-Catholic writer who contends that there is no hint of a distinction between "clergy and laity" in the New Testament. The argument between Catholics and Protestants over the origin of the distinction is of no interest to one who is neither Catholic nor Protestant, but merely a humble Christian. We have before demonstrated that all of God's people (laity) are his clergy (lot or inheritance). The distinction between the two which now exists in both Catholicism and Protestantism is without divine warrant, and is one of the marks of those of whom our Lord spoke, "Their heart is far from me; in vain they do worship me, teaching as doctrines the precepts of men" (Matt. 15: 8, 9). There is just as much scriptural authority for a pope as for a Protestant clergyman—and there is none!

That the "early fathers" may make reference to "bishops, priests and deacons," we will not deny, but that the *grandfathers,* the apostles, make any such distinction as Rome makes we emphatically deny. Nowhere in the Acts of Apostles, or in any of the writings of Paul, is the Greek term for priest, translated with any clerical bearing, as pertains to the Christian church. It is strange that Dr. O'Brien does not cite the passages in Acts or the Pauline epistles substantiating his claims.

The quotation from Clement does not prove what the priestly advocate wishes it to prove. Certainly the apostles appointed "bishops and deacons" in each congregation. But they did not appoint *"bishops, priests, and deacons."* The bishops were also called elders, pastors, presbyters, overseers, and shepherds. A plurality of such pastors were ordained in every congregation (Titus 1: 5; Acts 14: 23). The congregation at Philippi was composed of "saints with bishops and deacons" (Phil. 1: 1). Clement shows that such officers were placed in office by the apostles, "with the approval of the whole church." This is one "father" that Rome should be very quiet about, for the things he writes are in exact opposition to those which Rome practices. Where is the authority of this quotation from Clement for one priest over each parish, and a bishop over a multitude of churches?

A HIERARCHY

I have before me the citations of many early Fathers showing a clear recognition by the infant Church of the priesthood as a divinely established office, for the reception of which the sacrament of Orders was instituted. Space permits but the following one from St. Gregory of Nyssa (395) who reflects the mind of all the early writers. "The same power of the word," he says, "renders sublime and honorable the priest, who, by the newness of Ordination, has been singled out from the multitude; he who was yesterday one of the people suddenly becomes a commander, a presiding officer, a teacher of righteousness, and the dispenser of hidden mysteries." (Orat. in Bapt. Christi).

The Council of Trent declares that there is in the Catholic Church a divinely established hierarchy of bishops, priests, and deacons, and that bishops are superior to priests and possess the power of confirming and ordaining. (Sess. 23. Canons 6, 7.) Since Christ established the priesthood as a permanent institution He certainly conferred upon some priests, namely, bishops, the power of communicating the priesthood to others. It is evident from the New Testament that the Apostles were bishops, for it depicts them frequently as ordaining, which is the function characteristic of bishops. The episcopate is the completion of the priesthood.

The citations given do not show a clear recognition "by the infant churches of the priesthood as a divinely established office." Only two authorities are quoted. The first is Gregory of Nyssa who lived 350 years after the church was established, and had already departed from its original pattern. A graduate of the catechetical school at Alexandria, he had absorbed the allegorical interpretations and bold speculations of Origen who was formerly head of the seminary. The quotation given does not show what the infant church thought, but represents the views current in the days of Gregory of Nyssa, long after the Nicene creed was written. If the priest wished to show what the infant church believed, why did he not quote from the New Testament scriptures? An infant that is 359 years old is quite a lusty youngster.

The second authority mentioned is the Council of Trent, which was convened by Pope Paul III in 1545, and after several disputes and adjournments, was again assembled by Pius IV, Jan. 8, 1562. Its twenty-five sessions constituted so many debates in which the decrees were passed by a majority of the delegates, of which the Italians were more numerous than all of the other nations together. The above citation from the twenty-third session of this group holds no authority for a Christian. We are interested in a "Thus saith the Lord," and not a decree of a human synod passed by a majority vote. The witnesses being worthless, the testimony offered relative to "A Hierarchy" is also worthless.

It is not evident from the New Testament that the apostles were bishops. Paul, who ordained elders, was not a bishop, for among the qualifications he lists as essential to a man desiring the office of a bishop, one requirement was that he be "the husband of one wife" (1 Tim. 3: 2; Titus 1: 6). Paul was not a married man (1 Cor. 7: 8; 9: 5). There is not one iota of proof that "the function characteristic of bishops" is ordaining. The word bishop means "an overseer, a superintendent." One might fulfill his function as a bishop and never ordain anyone. Dr. O'Brien is arguing from modern Catholicism backward, instead of from New Testament Christianity forward. The Roman Catholic hierarchy is without a divine leg upon which to stand. It is a mushroom growth of an ecclesiastical seed, planted in hierarchical ambition, fertilized by superstition, and nurtured on pride.

SUPERIORITY OF EPISCOPATE

St. Ignatius of Antioch (98-117) describes the three orders of bishops, priests and deacons, and points out clearly the divine origin of the episcopate and its superiority over the priesthood. "The college of presbyters," he writes, "adheres to the bishop as the strings to a lyre." (Ad Eph., 4: 1) "Where the bishop is, there let the multitude (of believers) be; even as where Jesus Christ is, there is the Catholic Church." (Ad Smyr., 8: 2)

The so-called Apostolic Fathers are Clement, Barnabas, Hermas, Ignatius, Polycarp and Papias. Of these, Ignatius was the first to even suggest the idea of the Episcopate. Enroute to a martyr's death he is alleged to have written seven letters addressed to Ephesians, Magnesians, Trollians, Philadelphians, Smyrnaeans, Romans, and to Polycarp. The above quoted portions are from the first and fifth of these epistles. In addition to these, an excerpt from the letter to the Magnesians, reads, "Your bishop presides in the place of God, and your presbyters in the place of the assembly of the apostles. Ye are nothing without your bishop."

One is made to question why Ignatius is forced to go to such extravagant lengths in defending the office of the bishop. Is it because that office was a newly invented one, which the disciples were reluctant to recognize? Why did Ignatius not cite the teaching of the holy apostles to bolster his contention? The answer is that the apostolic writings know nothing of "the bishop."

Even so, there are several things which Rome might well consider in the writing of Ignatius. In spite of the fact that his letters indicate a well-defined deviation from apostolic teaching, it is noticeable that there is no trace of episcopal authority extending beyond a single community or congregation. The idea of a bishop over numerous churches, or a diocese, was not known as yet.

Neither does Ignatius rest the idea of episcopal authority on the same ground as that which Rome now attempts to defend it. The contention now is that the bishops are successors to the apostles, but Ignatius clearly assigned that status to the presbyters. Of the seven epistles acknowledged by Eusebius, there are two Greek recensions, a longer and shorter one, with the latter generally accepted as genuine. In both of them several glosses are apparent and it is evident they have suffered from alterations. To what extent they may be authentic is questionable, but in any event, they are not inspired and cannot be a true measure of God's plan for the congregations of saints.

CELIBACY OF THE CLERGY

"Why don't priests marry?" is one of the questions most frequently asked by non-Catholics. The celibacy of the clergy is not a precept of the divine or natural law, nor a dogma of the Catholic Church. It is simply a disciplinary regulation of the Western Church, imposed with a view to the more effective discharge of the priestly duties and a closer approximation to the ideal of our great High Priest, Jesus Christ. "He that is without a wife," says St. Paul, "is solicitous for the things that belong to the Lord, how he may please God. But he that is with a wife is solicitous for the things of the world, how he may please his wife; and he is divided." (I Cor. 7: 32, 33)

During the first three centuries there was no law of the Church enforcing celibacy. Clement of Alexandria speaks of married priests and deacons, and the historian Socrates refers to a married episcopate in the Eastern Churches. To this day the secular clergy in the Greek Catholic Church, that is, the Church in communion with Rome, are married, though the bishops are celibates. In short, it is not a question of dogma, but solely of ecclesiastical discipline. On this particular point of discipline there exists a difference, between the Church of the West and that of the East, though both are united in the acceptance of the dogma proclaiming the divine origin of the priesthood.

Inasmuch as the above has nothing to do with the subject of the origin of special priesthood, it requires but little attention. It is plainly admitted that celibacy of the clergy is not a precept of divine or natural law, therefore it originated as an arbitrary regulation of the hierarchy. It needs to be remarked that on one hand Rome raises matrimony to the rank of "a sacrament"; then refuses it to her clergy. She first exalts it in a sense which He does not justify. It is still true that marriage is to be held "in honor among all" (Heb. 13: 4), and that one symptom of apostasy is manifested "through the pretensions of liars whose consciences are seared, who forbid marriage and enjoin abstinence from foods" (1 Tim. 4: 2, 3).

A SUBLIME OFFICE

Having presented the evidence from Scripture and the writings of the early Fathers as to the divine origin of the priesthood and its essential powers, let us now briefly consider the dignity of the office, and the benefits which accrue to human society from its exercise. The priest is singled out by God who chooses him to be His ambassador to men. The words which Christ addressed to the Apostles at the Last Supper may be applied to all His priests: "You have not chosen me, but I have chosen you; and have appointed you, that you should go, and should bring forth fruit; and your fruit should remain." (John, 15: 16). It was this same divine teaching which St. Paul reechoed when he declared to the Hebrews: "Neither doth any man take the honor to himself, but he that is called by God, as Aaron was." (Heb. 5: 4).

The priest is called by God not only into the line of Aaron, into the tribe of Levi, into the family of Samuel, into the priesthood of Melchisedech, but into the discipleship of Jesus Christ. He is made a member of that goodly company of disciples whose sound has gone forth unto the ends of the earth. Throughout nineteen hundred years they have borne the teachings of the Divine Master into every race and every land from the frozen snows of the Arctic to the burning sands of the Sahara, and even unto the far distant shores washed by the waves of the Australasian seas.

We might well stop our review at this juncture seeing that the very first sentence of the above has been proven false. We have examined the evidence from

Scripture and the early fathers, and found it not only inconclusive in sustaining Rome's postulate, but actually opposed to the idea of the divine origin of a special priesthood. Since the office exists without heavenly warrant it is a usurper in the religious realm, and can only do ultimate harm instead of good to society from its exercise.

No one living today is an ambassador of God, a minister plenipotentiary. The words which Christ spoke to his chosen ambassadors *as apostles* apply to no other persons. That which he spoke to them as *disciples* may apply to all disciples as such, but the apostolic commission and regulations apply exclusively to eye witnesses of Jesus Christ, which the priests today cannot possibly be. The statement of Paul in Hebrews 5: 4 which the writer quotes, has direct reference to our Lord, as the following verse indicates, "So also Christ did not exalt himself to be made a high priest but was appointed by him" (i.e. God). The God of heaven did not appoint parish priests as he selected Aaron and Christ.

Perhaps no greater collection of Romish trivia could be found in the same space than that which asserts the Catholic priests are "called into the line of Aaron, into the tribe of Levi, into the family of Samuel, into the priesthood of Melchisedech, into the discipleship of Jesus Christ." It is evident that those who are in the "tribe of Levi" cannot serve God under the Christian dispensation as special priests, because there has been "a change in the priesthood, and necessarily a change in the law as well" (Heb. 7: 12). Our Lord who was of the order of Melchizedek was not of the line of Aaron, the tribe of Levi, or of the family of Samuel. "For the one of whom these things are spoken belonged to another tribe, from which no one has ever served at the altar. For it is evident that our Lord was descended from Judah, and in connection with that tribe Moses said nothing about priests" (Heb. 7: 13, 14).

Now in order to have their robes, incense, holy water, anointing oil and unbloody sacrifices, the Romish priests have to claim "the line of Aaron, and the tribe of Levi." But if they do that, they must give up the priesthood of Melchizedek (Heb. 7: 11). If they claim the priesthood of Melchizedek they must surrender all of their pomp, pageantry and ritual, for these belong to the Levitical priesthood. They cannot claim to be members of both for if so they have no connection with our high priest, seeing He was not of the line of Aaron, or the tribe of Levi. The whole truth is that the Romish priests are neither of Levi nor Melchizedek, but represent spiritual parasites, fungus growths upon the religious world. The desperate attempt to find scriptural justification for the existence of this ignoble hierarchy must end in despair.

THE POWER TO PARDON

It is possible for a priest in the great religio-politico institution designated the Roman Catholic Church to utter words of truth. He may have an unscriptural motive in his statement, or he may intend an application foreign to that conveyed by his words, but the statement as made may be factual. A good example is the following:

CHRIST IS WITH THEM

"Behold!" said Christ, "I am with you all days even to the consummation of the world." With these words echoing in their ears, the Apostles went out into the countries of the then known world, preaching the gospel fearlessly to every creature. They quailed not before the lions in the Roman arena, nor before the pitch and tar with which they were to be burned alive to illumine the gladiatorial contests of the Romans. Why? Because they realized that they were speaking not in their own names, but in the name of Jesus Christ. Because they realized that they were His divinely appointed ambassadors, clothed by the Master with plenipotentiary power to speak and teach in His name. That is why St. Paul was able to say with truth: "Let a man so regard us as ministers of Christ and dispensers of the mysteries of God." (1 Cor. 4: 1).

The paragraph as quoted is absolutely correct, but the application to a modern priestcraft is not correct. We endorse the statement just as it stands, because it is proven to be true by both the word of the Lord and history. But the Romish priests are not the successors of the apostles and any attempted application of the statement to them is delusive and deceptive.

POWER OF PARDONING

The second great power of the priestly office is that of pardoning. When the priest raises aloft his right hand and pronounces the words of pardon over the sinner in the tribunal of confession, the shackles are torn from the soul of the penitent. The priest pardons as effectively as if the words fell from the lips of Christ. It is a power which transcends that of kings and emperors. The power of kings is over the bodies of men. But they stand impotent before the kingdom of the soul. The hand of the priest reaches up beyond the horizon of the sky, and with golden keys unlocks the treasury of God's mercy and forgiveness and applies them to the souls of men.

The priest preserves inviolate the secrecy of the confessional even at the cost of life itself. Under no circumstances does he ever reveal the slightest imperfection breathed into his ear in confession.

The theory of Rome is that the secret confessional is a court of justice, over which the priest presides as jurist, jury, attorney and executioner. To this court the penitent comes, discloses his acts and receives his sentence, or pronouncement of innocence.

Bossuet, the Bishop of Meaux, in his *Exposition*, page 33, said: "We believe that Jesus Christ has been pleased that those who have submitted themselves to the government of the Church by baptism, and who have since violated the laws of the Gospel, should come and submit themselves to the judgment of the same Church, *in the tribunal of penance*, where she exercises the power which is given her, of remitting and retaining sins (Matt. 18: 18, John 20: 23). . . . This penitential court of justice being so necessary a curb to licentiousness—

so plentiful a source of wise admonition—so sensible a consolation of souls afflicted by their sins, when their absolution is not only declared in general terms, but when they are in reality absolved by the authority of Jesus Christ, after a particular examination and knowledge of the case."

This Catholic authority states that there is a tribunal of penance, that it constitutes a court of justice, that here violators submit to the judgment of the church, and absolution is granted by the authority of Christ, and such absolution is given only after examination of the case. Thus, each parish priest is judge and jury, and from his decision no appeal can be made. He is a *local* priest but the *supreme* court.

To sustain our statement we quote from *Grounds of Catholic Doctrine*, page 22: "Christ has made the pastors of His Church His judges in the court of conscience, with commission and authority to bind or loose, to forgive or to retain sins, to the merits of the cause and the disposition of the penitents. Now, as no judge can pass sentence without having a full knowledge of the cause, which cannot be had in this kind of causes which regards men's consciences, but by their own confession, it clearly follows, that He who has made the pastors of the Church the judges of men's consciences, has also laid an obligation upon the faithful to lay open the state of their consciences to them, if they hope to have their sins remitted."

The confession booth is thus a secret court in which a man probes the conscience of another and passes sentence upon the victim of error. Such a thing is unknown to the Holy Scriptures. But what passages are twisted and wrested to uphold auricular confession?

One is James 5: 16, about which *Grounds of Catholic Doctrine* has this to say: " 'Confess therefore your sins one to another,' that is to the priests or elders of the church, whom the apostles ordered to be called for (verse 14)." An examination of the passage does not prove what Rome would like for it to prove. It is against auricular confession to a priest. In the first place, the elders are not priests in an official sense. After James gave instruction to call the elders in under certain circumstances, he does not say to confess your sins unto them, but rather, "Confess your sins one to another, and pray for one another." When one disciple of the Lord confesses his sin to another, it is one of God's priests confessing his error to another of God's priests, but the confession is mutual, just as the prayers are to be.

Another passage cited by Rome is Acts 19: 18: "Many also of those who were now believers came, confessing and divulging their practices." Instead of this being a secret confession whispered in privacy in a secluded booth, it was an open acknowledgment of practices which had previously been indulged, but which were now discovered to be in contravention of divine precepts. That this is true, is further suggested by the next verse which says, "And a number of those who practiced magical arts brought their books together and burned them *in the sight of all.*" Every text which Rome adduces for her confessional will be found under close scrutiny to apply to public confession and not to private or secret confession to a human tribunal.

The statement, "The priest pardons as effectively as if the words fell from the lips of Christ" borders upon blasphemy. It is a pretentious, proud and arrogant assertion, but it is without any authority from God. Nowhere do the holy apostles ever hint at such a tribunal as that about which Rome prates. When the incestuous member at Corinth was determined to be guilty, the whole congregation when assembled, acted upon his case; when he repented the whole congregation was instructed to forgive and comfort him. But their forgiveness was for the reproach brought upon the congregation, and consisted of a remission of their own censure as evidenced in the act of formal exclusion from the group. Fornication is a sin against God and can only be forgiven by God. But, if auricular confession was the means of obtaining pardon, why did Paul not advise this both to the congregation and the penitent? If the apostles had such power, why did they not once refer to it? John declares, "If any man sin, we have an advocate with the Father, Jesus Christ the righteous" (1 John 2: 1). He does not say, "If any man sin, we have a judicial tribunal in which one may confess and receive absolution."

The hand of a priest can reach no higher than that of any humble supplicant. He has no golden key that is not afforded unto all alike. Every child of God is invited to "Have confidence to enter the sanctuary by the blood of Jesus, by the new and living way which He opened for us through the curtain of His flesh, and since we have a great high priest over the house of God, let us draw near with true heart in full assurance of faith, with our hearts sprinkled clean from an evil conscience and our bodies washed with pure water" (Heb. 10: 19-22). The golden key belongs to every immersed believer, for every such person is "a priest of God." Any special priest who claims exclusive right to unlock the treasury of God is a usurper and a pretentious despoiler of God's citizenry.

SEAL OF CONFESSION

The sacrifice which every Catholic priest stands ready to make to preserve this trust inviolate is illustrated by the following historical incident. In

1899 Father Dumoulin, a French priest, was charged with the crime of murder. The sexton had murdered and robbed a wealthy woman. To throw suspicion from himself he dipped the smoking revolver in the woman's blood and placed it in Father Dumoulin's room. Then to seal the lips of the priest, he went to confession to Father Dumoulin, accusing himself of the murder.

Circumstantial evidence pointed to the priest. Knowing how secure he was behind the sacramental seal, knowing that the priest could not open those lips to reveal the guilty person even to save his own life, the sexton gave testimony convicting the priest. He was given a life sentence worse than death—life imprisonment at hard labor on Devil's Island under the tropical sun, whither France sends her worst criminals. Suffering the loss of his good name, the ostracism of his friends and a public ignominy that was more painful than death itself, Father Dumoulin, like the good priest that he was, remained faithful to his trust.

For twenty-five years he toiled under the burning rays of the tropical sun among the outcasts of mankind, guarding ever the secret in his bosom. In those twenty-five years he saw his mother die of a broken heart, carrying to her grave the blight of her son's imprisonment. Twenty-five years of grinding convict toil had left him with grey hairs, a face deep lined, a body broken and bent, on the edge of the grave.

CLEARED AFTER 25 YEARS

In a wretched hovel in a slum district in Paris a man lying on a bare cot is calling hysterically for a priest before he dies. As the priest enters, he shouts aloud: "I am guilty of the murder for which Father Dumoulin was condemned. I sealed his lips with confession and threw the guilt on him." Unwilling to face his God with that foul crime upon his soul, he seeks forgiveness through the very agency of confession whose inviolable secrecy he perverted to convict an innocent priest.

What a tardy retribution that could not undo those

> **twenty-five years of mental torture, that could not recall the dead from their graves, nor reveal to them his innocence. And yet that is precisely what every priest in Christendom would willingly undergo rather than reveal the tiniest venial sin breathed into his ear in confession. Such is the absolute, impenetrable and inviolable secrecy with which a priest guards the contents of every confession.**

This purely prejudicial material has not one thing to do with the issue. The title of the booklet by Dr. O'Brien is "The Priesthood: A Divine Institution." Does the fact that a priest refuses to reveal secrets breathed into his ear prove that the priesthood of Roman Catholicism is divinely ordained? Does it prove that auricular confession is an institution of heaven? Julius and Ethel Rosenberg, the condemned Communistic traitors, went to their death without revealing a single secret concerning their conspirators. Would this prove that Communism is a divine institution?

Can that be a divine institution which prompts men to lie and even do so under a solemn oath? Yet "the seal of confession" does just that. This is proven by an excerpt from the work of Rev. Peter Dens, D.D., on *"The Nature of Confession and Obligation of the Seal,"* as translated by the monk of La Trappe, E. Zosinius. At a meeting of the Roman Catholic prelates in Ireland, held on September 14, 1808, it was agreed that Dens' *"Complete Body of Theology"* was the best book extant on the subject. Let us note these quotations from it.

"What is the seal of sacramental confession?"

Answer: "It is the obligation or duty of concealing those things which are learned from sacramental confession."

"Can a case be given in which it is lawful to break the sacramental seal?"

Answer: "It cannot, though life be forfeited, or a

commonwealth be destroyed."

"What answer, then, ought a confessor to give when questioned concerning a truth which he knows from sacramental confession only?"

Answer: "He ought to answer, that he does not know it, and, if it be necessary, to confirm the same with an oath."

To deliberately falsify, and then to ask God to witness the lie as truth is certainly taking His name in vain. Yet we are asked to believe that such a system is heroic, courageous and commendatory. But the whole truth is that "the seal" can be broken. Liguori, the famed Catholic historian, quoted so frequently by Alexander Campbell in his debate with Right Rev. John B. Purcell, Bishop of Cincinnati, declares that "the seal" must not be broken lest the confession be rendered odious, but he also says that the confessor may secure licence of the penitent, and that such licence may be granted in writing or orally. Since the Roman Catholic is taught to regard the priest as God in the confessional, it is evident that to refuse to submit to a demand for such licence would be to fight against God, in his superstitious mind.

The writer mentions "the sacrifice which every Catholic priest stands ready to make to preserve the trust inviolate." Such a sacrifice does not prove that the truth itself is worthy. It may demonstrate the belief of the priest in his trust, and even show the consistency with which he views it, but that still does not establish the righteousness of the trust. The fact that a man is willing to die for a thing, does not prove the thing itself is true, although it may demonstrate that *he believes it* to be so. Men, like Horatius, might die as willingly for pagan gods, as Christians would for the true and living God.

"Then outspake brave Horatius,
The captain of the gate:
'To every man upon this earth
Death cometh soon or late.
And how can man die better
Than facing fearful odds
For the ashes of his fathers
And the temples of his gods?"

No account of suffering upon the part of a priest can establish the scripturality of auricular confession. It is a miserable imposture spawned during the darkest days of the world and religion, when the sun of intellect hid her face because of the pollutions of a profligate priesthood. It became a dogma and an obligatory practice of the Roman Church at the Lateran Council, in 1215 A.D., under Pope Innocent III. Not one trace of it, as a dogma, can be found prior to that year.

St. John Chrysostom, from whose celebrated works, Rome loves to quote, said in his homily on Psalm 50: "We do not request you to go confess your sins to any of your fellow-men, but only God."

In his Homily V, *De incomprehensibili De natura*, Vol. 1, he says: "Therefore I beseech you, always confess your sins to God! I, in no way, ask you to confess them to me. To God alone should you expose the wounds of your soul and from Him alone expect the cure. Go to Him, then, and you shall not be cast off, but healed. For, before you utter a single word, God knows your prayer."

It is questionable whether the priest undergoes any more mental torture than that which is suffered by a refined and modest woman who must be subjected to questioning and prodding relative to her innermost thoughts, and who is forced to disclose to a bachelor, the most intimate feelings she may not even mention to her own husband. The confessional box is a throne of priestly control where a man sits who has his finger on the pulsing heart and throbbing conscience of every member of a domestic circle, and who claims the very authority of God in releasing or retaining sins.

THE POWER TO CONSECRATE

It is in her claim that the priest has the power to consecrate, that Rome indulges in the language of blasphemy, claiming that the priest is equal in power to our Lord and speaks in the very voice of God. "Consecration" as Rome uses the term has to do with the alleged power to transmute the elements of bread and fruit of the vine into the actual body and blood of our Lord.

The Council of Trent declared: "By the consecration of the bread and wine a change is wrought of the bread's whole substance into the substance of Christ our Lord's body, and of the wine's whole substance into the substance of His blood, which change has been by the Holy Catholic Church suitably and properly called Transubstantiation" (Session 13, Chapter 4).

In explanation of this language, Rome says: "By the substance of bread we mean its very essence, that internal, invisible something which, itself devoid of color, shape, weight, taste, etc. supports the qualities or accidents which are perceived by the senses. Transubstantiation therefore, means that when Jesus Christ, at the Last Supper, pronounced the words, 'This is my body; this is my blood,' the Son of God by His omnipotent power transubstantiated or changed, the substance of the bread and wine into His living flesh; so that no bread or wine whatsoever remained, but Himself, body, blood, soul and divinity, under their appearances. So in like manner, every day at Mass, the priest, acting in the name of Christ pronounces the same words, and God effects the same change" (*The Question Box,* Conway, page 417).

POWER OF CONSECRATION

> **The third great power of the priestly office is the climax of all. It is the power of consecrating. "No act is greater," says St. Thomas "than the consecration of the sacred body of Christ." In this essential phase of the sacred ministry, the power of the priest is not surpassed by that of the bishop, the archbishop, the cardinal or the pope. Indeed it is equal to that of Jesus Christ. For in this role the priest speaks with the voice and authority of God himself.**

Since it is affirmed that this is a great power belonging to the priestly office, and that it represents the grand climax of all sacerdotal demonstrations, it will be in order for us to investigate it to the extent our limited space will allow. Rome not only teaches that the bread is the real body of our Lord and the cup is His real blood, but she demands under threat of anathema that her superstitious followers also believe that each particle of bread when separated, and each drop of the wine, is in itself *the entire Christ.*

The Council of Trent says: "*Canon 3:*—If any one shall deny that the venerated sacrament of the Eucharist, entire Christ is contained in each kind, and in each several particles of either kind, when separated, let him be accursed." If the consecrated bread became divided into ten thousand crumbs, each crumb would in and of itself be the entire Christ or if the consecrated fruit of the vine became separated into uncounted drops, each drop would be the entire Christ.

And if this were not too much for those who were nurtured on the pap of gullibility and blind credulity, the Catholic must also believe that he crunches between his teeth the very bones and nerves of the Son of Man. "Not only the true body of Christ, and whatever appertains to the true mode of existence of a body, and the bones and nerves, but also that entire Christ is contained in the sacrament."

Upon what foundation does this monstrous fabrication, with all of its ramifications, find rest? Upon the simple words of our Master, "This is my body; this is my blood," and the instruction, "Do this in memory of me." How did the apostles understand these words? They were all Jews, who knew it was contrary to the law to drink the blood of animals, much more human blood. They were rigorous in their observance of the law with reference to eating *the flesh* of only certain kinds of animals. They would have abhorred the very idea of cannibalism, the eating of human flesh, bones and veins. Yet, not a word escaped their lips upon this night. The impetuous Peter asked no question about the Lord's statement. Surely they knew that the living and real Christ was giving them only a memorial consisting of two elements. They did not believe that the living Christ took His literal body, and dividing it into the numerous parts, made of each a literal and *entire Christ.*

Can the words upon which Rome stakes so much, be understood figuratively? If I hand you a photograph saying, "This is my mother," do you conclude that I mean that the piece of sensitized photographic paper is my mother in a literal sense? If I walk through a public park with a friend, and he points to a statute, saying, "This is George Washington," do I suppose that he means the piece of bronze is the literal general of the Revoluntionary Army? Did Jesus ever use symbolic language with reference to himself? He said, "I am the vine" (John 15: 1). Shall we conclude that he was transmuted into a grapevine, and that each twig when separate was the *entire Christ?* He said, "I am the door" (John 10: 9). Did he infer that he was a literal door?

Even Rome has difficulty in explaining her position, insomuch that some of her outstanding scholars recognize the problem. The Catholic bishop, Tonstal, admitted: "Of the manner and means of the real presence, how it might be either by transubstantiation or otherwise, perhaps it had been better to leave any one, who would be curious, to his own opinion, as before the Council of Lateran it was left" (*The Eucharist,* Book 1, page 46).

Cardinal de Alliaco said: "That manner and meaning which supposeth the substance of bread to remain, is possible; neither is it contrary to reason, nor to the authority of the Scriptures, nay it is more easy and more reasonable to conceive, if it could only accord with the Church."

The very language of the apostle detailing the observance of the feast, proves that it is a memorial for one *who is absent,* and not a recognition of the bodily presence of that person. The expression, "Do this in remembrance of me" surely points to the fact that the one thus commemorated is not present. Why should one do something *in remembrance* of Jesus, if the *real Christ* is present in body, blood, bones and nerves? Moreover, we are told that in eating and drinking, we "proclaim the Lord's death *until he comes.*" Does this not indicate that He has not already literally come? If the real Christ is upon the altar, and visible to the communicants, as Rome teaches, how can the priest explain the term "until he comes"?

In the very same connection which Rome declares

Jesus consecrated the bread and wine by saying, "This is my body; this is my blood," He also took the cup saying, "This cup *is the new testament.*" He did not say that it represented or adumbrated the new testament. He said it was the new testament. Is this to be taken literally? Rome does not believe so. She accepts it as a figure of speech. By the same identical reasoning, we accept what our Lord said about the bread and fruit of the vine figuratively.

The host (bread) is made of wheat flour and water and is unleavened. It is baked with heat. Rome teaches that when the priest utters the words "Hoc est corpus meum" this unleavened bread is converted into the real Christ. Thus a god is produced by the work of men's hands, and men bow and acknowledge the host is "God over all" when it is elevated by the priest. This is contrary to the revelation of God, which amply shows that nothing can become God which is made with men's hands. Demetrius said, "You see and hear that not only at Ephesus but almost throughout all Asia this Paul has persuaded and turned away a considerable company of people, saying that gods made with hands are not gods" (Acts 19: 26).

The prophet Isaiah condemns those who "bow down to the work of their hands, to what their own fingers have made" (2: 8). The sweet psalmist of Israel declared,

> "The idols of the nations are silver and gold,
> The work of men's hands" (Psalm 135: 15).

The Romish priest cannot deny that the wafer which he presumes to consecrate is made by the hands of men, and that he teaches that it is converted into very Christ and is worshipped as God.

When the priest pronounces the tremendous words of consecration, he reaches up into the heavens,

brings Christ down from his throne, and places Him upon our altar to be offered up again as the victim for the sins of man. It is greater power than that of monarchs and potentates. It is greater than that of saints and angels, greater than that of Seraphim and Cherubim. Indeed it is greater even than the power of the Virgin Mary. For, while the Blessed Virgin was the human agency by which Christ became incarnate a single time, the priest brings Christ down from Heaven, and renders Him incarnate on the altar as the eternal Victim for the sins of man—not once but a thousand times! The priest speaks and lo! Christ, the eternal and omnipotent God, bows His head in humble obedience to the priest's command.

The above paragraph is a positive denial of the truth as revealed in God's Word. It is a clear demonstration of the extent to which a boastful priestcraft will go to delude and deceive a superstitious following. Let us note the fallacious reasoning in the boastful assertions.

Does the priest "reach up into the heavens, and bring Christ down from His throne?" The inspired apostle declares, "The righteousness based on faith says, Do you say in your heart, 'Who will ascend into heaven?' (that is to bring Christ down)" (Rom. 10:6). Surely, according to Roman Catholic admission, they do not have the righteousness which is based on faith. Jesus was elevated to His throne by the power of God. Shall he be removed from it by the power of men? "We have such a high priest, one who is seated at the right hand of the throne of the Majesty in heaven" (Heb. 8: 1). Now Christ cannot be on His throne, if he is brought "from His throne" by every Catholic priest; He cannot be in heaven if He is "brought down" by one who "reaches up into the heavens." But since our "hope that enters into the inner shrine behind the curtain, where Jesus has gone as a forerunner on our behalf"

(Heb. 6: 19, 20) is predicated upon His remaining "exalted above the heavens" (Heb. 7: 26) no Roman Catholic can have the hope of eternal life during the time that the priest is "consecrating the Eucharist."

Can the priest place Christ "upon an altar to be offered again as the victim for the sins of men?" We answer in an emphatic negative. Such a preposterous theory gives the lie to the whole plan of God. To justify her special priesthood, Rome has to run counter to the divine scheme of the ages. Jesus Christ is no longer "a victim for the sins of man." "He has no need, like those high priests, to offer up sacrifices daily, first for his own sins and then for those of the people; he did this *once for all* when he offered up himself" (Heb. 7: 27). Christ is not a daily victim; He does not have to suffer repeatedly. He does not require to be sacrificed daily for sins. "Nor was it to offer himself *repeatedly,* as the high priest enters the Holy Place yearly with the blood not his own; for then he would have had to suffer *repeatedly* since the foundation of the world. But as it is, he has appeared *once for all* at the end of the age to put away sin by the sacrifice of himself" (Heb. 9: 25, 26).

Notice the word "again" in the priestly language which says, Christ is "offered up *again* as the victim for the sins of man." Here is a good place to hinge the controversy between the false claims of Rome and the truth of heaven. Roman Catholicism teaches that Jesus must be offered *again*—"not once but a thousand times." The Bible says, "But when Christ had offered for all time a *single sacrifice* for sins, he sat down at the right hand of God, then to wait until his enemies should be made a stool for his feet. For by a *single offering* he has perfected for all time those who are sanctified" (Heb. 10: 12-14). Rome says "*again*"; the

Bible say "only once." Rome says *"a thousand times"*; the Bible says "a single sacrifice for all times."

The boasted power over monarchs, potentates, saints and angels, is nothing but a myth, a fictitious fancy of a fertile, ingenious priestcraft, to make serfs and vassals of their fellowmen. "Priestcraft in all ages and all nations has been the same; its nature is one and that nature is essentially evil; its object is self-gratification and self-aggrandizement; the means it uses—the basest frauds, the most shameless delusions, practiced on the popular mind for the acquisition of power; and that power once gained, the most fierce and bloody exercise of it, in order to render it at once lawful and perpetual. Nothing is so servilely mean in weakness, so daring in assumption, so arrogant in command: earth, Heaven, the very throne and existence of God himself, being used as but the tools of its designs, and appealed to with horrible impudence in the most shameless of its lies." (*History of Priestcraft in All Ages and Nations,* by William Howitt, pages 14, 15).

Does Christ "bow His head in humble obedience to the priest's command"? Such insolence should cause every humble member of the Roman Catholic Church to tremble in every fiber at the thought of upholding such a blasphemous institution. God raised Christ from the dead "and made him sit at his right hand in the heavenly places, far above all rule and authority and power and dominion, and above every name that is named, not only in this age but also in that which is to come; and he has put all things under his feet and has made him head over all things for the church" (Eph. 1: 20-22). Our Lord bows His head at the command of no man. He is the Commander, not the commanded. He is not to humbly obey the dictates of any man, but all men must humbly obey His dictates.

The sacrifice of our Lord has been made. It cannot be repeated. Once He was crucified; now He is glorified. Once He was humiliated; now He is exalted. He cannot be humiliated again. "Being found in human form He humbled himself and became obedient unto death, even death on a cross. Therefore God has highly exalted him and bestowed on him the name which is above every name, that at the name of Jesus every knee should bow, in heaven and on earth and under the earth" (Phil. 2: 8, 9). The idea that a man on earth can reach up to heaven and take Jesus from His throne, and once more debase Him as a victim for sins, is horrifying to one who really believes in God. Truly it can be said, "They then commit apostasy, since they crucify the Son of God on their own account and hold him up to contempt" (Heb. 6: 6).

The *Roman Missal* says, "If the priest vomit the Eucharist, if the species appear entire, let them be reverently swallowed, unless sickness arise: for then let the consecrated species be cautiously separated and laid up in some sacred place, till they are corrupted; and afterwards let them be cast into the sacrarium" (*Roman Missal,* Mechlin, 1840). If you remember that the Romish teaching is that the consecrated bread is *entire Christ,* the abominable thought that Christ may be vomited up by a priest, who must thereupon rescue Him from the vomit and swallow Him again, unless nausea results, whereupon the entire Christ is to be fished out of the mess and laid up until corrupted, should be enough to turn the stomachs of all believers. Even the Pagan Roman soldiers did not subject the body of God's Son to more profane treatment than that required of the Romish priests.

As a further degradation, the common members of the Catholic Church were given the prayer which follows: "May thy body, O Lord, which I have received, and thy blood which I have drunk, cleave to my bowels, and grant that no stain of sin remain in me, who have been fed with this pure and holy sacrament. Who liveth and reigneth forever and ever. Amen." Is it possible that the literal body of our Lord should cling to the bowels of a man on earth, seeing that He is Lord of heaven and earth?

Of what sublime dignity is the office of the Christian priest who is thus privileged to act as the ambassador and the vicegerent of Christ on earth. He continues the essential ministry of Christ—he teaches the faithful with the authority of Christ, he pardons the penitent sinner with the power of Christ, he offers up again the same sacrifice of adoration and atonement which Christ offered on Calvary. No wonder that the name which spiritual writers are especially fond of applying to the priest is that of "alter Christus." For the priest is and should be another Christ. The priesthood is a sublime ministry, more meet for angels than for weak and sinful men. Truly indeed did Isaiah proclaim with prophetic insight six hundred years before Christ the grandeur of the Christian priesthood in these inspired words: "How beautiful on the mountains are the feet of him that bringeth good tidings and that preacheth peace; of him that showeth forth good, that preacheth salvation, that saith to Sion: Thy God shall reign" (Isaiah 52: 7).

We have shown by indisputable testimony that Romish priests are not ambassadors or vicegerents of Christ. We have established it as factual that they are not authoritative teachers, they cannot pardon sinners, and cannot offer up the sacrifice of Christ. These are the foundations of the hierarchical priestcraft, and we have swept them all away. Any power claimed by the priests on the basis of the Catholic contention is usurpation, and without divine warrant. Every child of God is a priest. Any person claiming special sacerdotal powers is a religious counterfeiter.

The priest is not "alter Christus"—another Christ.

There is one Christ. "Then if any one says to you 'Lo, here is the Christ!' or 'There he is!' do not believe it. For *false Christs* and false prophets will arise and show great signs and wonders, so as to lead you astray, if possible, even the elect" (Matt. 24: 23, 24). "For although there may be so-called gods in heaven or on earth—as indeed there are many 'gods' and many 'lords'—yet for us there is one God, the Father, from whom are all things and for whom we exist, and one Lord, Jesus Christ, through whom are all things and through whom we exist" (1 Cor. 8: 5, 6).

The apostle speaks of rebellion in which "the man of lawlessness is revealed, the son of perdition, who opposes and exalts himself against every so-called god or object of worship, so that he takes his seat in the temple of God, proclaiming himself to be God" (2 Thess. 2: 3, 4). We deny that the priest is and should be "another Christ." This is the language of apostasy, a part of the bold effrontery with which men are silenced and the voice of conscience is stricken dumb. The words of Isaiah were not spoken of a covetous, pretentious and ambitious clergy, but of humble preachers of the gospel as shown by the fulfillment in Romans 10: 14, 15. This is but another sample of the twisting of God's Word to justify an unholy and ungodly system by which men are exploited for gain.

PRIESTHOOD AND WORSHIP

It is the position of Rome that worship to God must be dependent upon a special clergy. This negates the purpose of God as respects the Christian dispensation, and takes the world back to the shadowy representations of the Jewish dispensation. It belongs to the "weak and beggarly elemental spirits" which enslave men (Gal. 4: 9) and from which we were freed by Him who was "born of woman, born under the law."

ALTAR AND PRIEST

Is it not apparent to every person, regardless of religious affiliation, who has followed this discussion with an open mind, that the Christian priesthood is an institution founded by Jesus Christ whereby men receive the power and authority to preach the gospel, to reconcile sinners and to offer sacrifice to the Most High? When Luther discarded the office of the priesthood, the confessional as a tribunal for the reconciliation of sinners and the altar with its august Sacrifice of the Mass disappeared. Now in the churches of our separated brethren there remain but the four bare walls and a pulpit. While the highest element of worship, the offering of sacrifice has completely vanished, even the other elements of worship are fast disappearing. Listen to the words addressed by Dr. Edmund S. Conklin to the ministers of our country: "After no small amount of observation, reading, and careful inquiry, I am forced to the conclusion that worship as a religious exercise is disappearing from Protestant Churches." (*The Disappearance of Wor-*

ship, The Christian Century, July 11, 1934).

Is it not apparent that this decay of worship in the Churches of our non-Catholic friends is due primarily to their abandonment of the priestly office? Is it not also apparent that the great decline in church attendance deplored by ministers throughout the counry is traceable to the discarding of the priesthood and the consequent disappearance of sacrifice and worship? More and more such churches are ceasing to be temples for the worship of God and are becoming lecture halls for the discussion of political, social and economic problems. But man does not live by bread alone. In the unfathomable depths of his nature, he strives now, as in the days of Cain and Abel and of Melchisedech, to offer sacrifice and worship to his God and Maker. Deep still calleth unto deep.

In the priesthood of the Catholic Church he will find a divinely established agency, through which that deep and ineradicable hunger of his nature will find adequate satisfaction. In that Church the searcher after truth will find not only preaching and prayer and the singing of hymns, but more than that—altar and priest, worship and sacrifice. For in the memory of the priest within that Church there echo the solemn words addressed by Jesus Christ to His first priests, the Apostles, at the Last Supper: "Do ye this in commemoration of me." In faithful compliance with that divine command, the priest offers up each day in all the countries of the world the august Sacrifice of the Mass saying the words of the psalmist: "I will take the chalice of salvation and I will call upon the name of the Lord."

We are sure that if the Romish priest could make mere assertion to act as positive proof his arguments would sound weighty and convincing. However, it must now be apparent to every person regardless of religious affiliation, that Jesus Christ founded no special priesthood possessed of the powers which are claimed by the hierarchy. On the contrary even Roman Catho-

lics who are honest, if they were permitted to read our dissertation, would conclude that the priesthood which lords it over their minds does so with no trace of scriptural warrant.

Men need not depend upon a clergy for power and authority to preach the gospel. This is an inalienable right of every citizen of the kingdom of priests. Rome claims that the apostles were the first priests and were so constituted to enable them to preach the gospel. But in Acts 8: 1, we read that "a great persecution arose against the church in Jerusalem; and they were all scattered abroad throughout the region of Judea and Samaria, *except the apostles.*" Verse 4 declares, "Now those who were scattered abroad went about preaching the word." If they were all scattered except the apostles, and it was those who were scattered who did the preaching, then it appears that "preaching the word" is the duty of every disciple.

The apostles did not forbid this preaching by others or claim an exclusive right to do it. Instead "when the apostles which were at Jerusalem heard that Samaria had received the word of God, they sent to them Peter and John." These two merely commended and confirmed the preaching done by non-apostolic labor. Nor can we help remarking that Peter did not do the sending. He was one of two men "sent by the apostles." Where is the vaunted papal authority about which Rome boasts for the "see of Peter"?

Again it is said, "Those who were scattered because of the persecution that arose over Stephen traveled as far as Phenicia and Antioch speaking the word to none except the Jews. But there were some of them, men of Cyprus and Cyrene, who on coming to Antioch spoke to the Greeks also, preaching the Lord Jesus. And the hand of the Lord was with them, and a great number that believed turned to the Lord" (Acts 11: 19-21). When news of this came to the ears of the Church in Jerusalem, they sent Barnabas to Antioch, not to forbid them to preach, for "when he came and saw the grace of God, he was glad; and he exhorted them all to remain faithful to the Lord with steadfast purpose." The proclamation of the gospel message is not the right of an exclusive caste. "Let him that heareth, say, Come."

Martin Luther did not discard the office of priesthood. He merely restored the scriptural idea regarding it, and assayed to give it to its rightful owners. Luther declared, "It has been said that the pope, the bishops, the priests, and all those who people the covenants form the spiritual or ecclesiastical state; and that the princes, the nobility, the citizens, and peasants, form the secular or lay estate. This is a fine story. Let no persons, however, be startled at it. All Christians belong to the spiritual estate, and there is no other difference between them than that arising from the function which they discharge. We have all one baptism, one faith; and this it is which constitutes the spiritual man. The unction, the tonsure, ordination, consecration by the bishop or the pope, may make a hypocrite, but never a spiritual man. We are all consecrated priests by baptism, as Saint Peter says, 'Ye are priests and kings,' although it does not belong to all to exercise such offices, for no one can take that which is common to all without the consent of the community."

Certainly the restoration of the idea of a kingdom of priests, all of whom are upon an equality as pertains to priesthood, would destroy the idea of a tribunal of conscience in which one elevates himself to the place where he can assess penalties and act as a supreme judge over others. There is but one high priest, who alone is able to forgive sins, and unto Him appeal must be made. "There is one lawgiver and judge, he who is able to save and to destroy" (James 4: 12).

As to the subject of the mass, Martin Luther said in the Augsburg Confession: "But as the mass, prior to this time, was abused in various ways; as it is clear, that an annual traffic was made out of it, that it was bought and sold, and that it was celebrated for the most part in all churches for the sake of money, such abuse had been repeatedly censured, even before this time by individuals of learning and piety. Now, as the ministers among us have preached concerning this thing, and the priests have been reminded of the terrible menaces which should justly move every Christian, that whoever partakes of the Sacrament unworthily, is guilty of the body and blood of Christ (1 Cor. 11: 27) in consequence of this, these sordid and solitary masses, which hitherto have been celebrated out of compulsion, for the sake of money and preferments, have ceased in our churches."

Philip Melancthon, brilliant young friend of Luther, in his "*Apology for the Augsburg Confession*" says: "Now, as no one under the Old Testament obtained remission of sins through the sacrifices, they having only signified the one sacrifice of Christ, it follows that there is only one offering, namely, Christ, who made payment and satisfaction for the sins of the whole world. In the New Testament, consequently, there is no sacrifice to be made as a recompense for sin, except only the death of Christ, who was offered once upon the cross. When they therefore assert that under the New Testament there must be a priest to offer sacrifice, this can be conceded with reference to Christ alone. The whole Epistle to the Hebrews strongly urges and confirms this view. It would really be setting up another mediator besides Christ, were we to admit any other satisfaction for sin, or any reconciliation but the death of Christ."

He further states: "Our antagonists cannot produce a particle of proof from the Scripture in confirmation of these dreams and fables, which they preach with the greatest assurance, although without the authority of the church or the Fathers. They are ungodly, perverse men, who knowingly reject and trample upon the plain truth of God." No wonder the reformatory movement aroused such a stir in men's hearts, with such courageous leaders in the vanguard of the army.

The statement regarding Protestants, that "in the churches of our separated brethren there remain but four bare walls and pulpit" deserves a few remarks. The dragon now speaks with the voice of a lamb. "Our separated brethren" of today were those branded as "infamous heretics" yesterday, and brutally treated and even killed by papal persecutions.

Dominus Dens says:

"Are heretics justly punished with death?"

Answer: "Saint Thomas answers in the affirmative because forgers of money, or others, disturbing the republic, are justly punished with death. Therefore, also heretics who are forgers of the faith, and, experience being the witness, greatly disturb the republic."

Pope Martin (1418) gave his approval to the Council of Constance in which heretics were condemned to be burned as "morbid sheep." Urban IV (1262) issued a bull for the appointment of officers to discharge the functions of the Inquisition against heretics. When Martin Luther laid down the proposition, "It is contrary to the will of God to burn heretics," Pope Leo X (1520) published a bull in which he condemned the proposition. Rome accommodates her tactics and methods to the time and place where she works. In an enlightened

America with religious freedom, she becomes tolerant, and speaks of "our separated brethren," but in places where she is in the majority, she shows her true tyrannical and despotic nature. Rome always has an axe to grind, and she turns the political grindstone to throw sparks in whatever direction will accomplish her purpose.

Yet there is a hint even in the accusation of Rome that Protestantism does not represent the restoration of simple New Testament Christianity. In the primitive church no pulpit was found. The early Christians sat around a table, the modern congregation sits before a pulpit. The first disciples met to minister to each other, the present day disciples meet to be ministered unto. For three hundred years the congregations owned no distinctive buildings, but met in upper rooms and in private homes. The familiar expression, "The church which is in thy house" was characteristic of the New Covenant epistles. In such simplicity was it necessary to have an elevated stand in each home? We do not condemn the use of a speaker's platform, but "the pulpit" has certain connotations. It has been borrowed from Rome by her "separated brethren" because they still have the false and unscriptural distinction between the clergy and the laity. The pulpit is the exclusive realm of a special caste. Humble saints are deemed unworthy of invading its sacred precincts unless by condescension, the priestly occupant invites one of the flock to share it with him to direct a prayer from its sacerdotal heights.

It is deemed a distinctive honor to "sit in the pulpit" by the side of "the minister." Mothers covet this glory for their sons, and simper with fawning gratitude when one of their offspring is invited to participate in the service. How tragic is this attitude which indicates so great a departure from the divine ideal of the regal priesthood with its absolute freedom of the platform protected for every faithful and able brother in the assembly of the saints.

Rome cannot conceive of a spiritual worship. She must walk by sight because she cannot walk by faith. She can no more visualize a congregation at worship without a visible, tangible altar and its officiating priest, than the Protestants can visualize a congregation at worship without a pulpit occupied by the minister. Yet the primitive church had neither of these. Both extremes are departures from the plan of God; both originated with and are perpetuated by the clergy. Neither system can restore to this world of sin the congregation as given by our Lord through His apostles.

Dr. Conklin is correct. Worship as a religious exercise is disappearing from Protestant churches. But it is not disappearing due to the lack of a special priestcraft. It is disappearing because of the Protestant counterpart thereof, the clergyman. Worship is not now a corporate action of the body in which all engage. It is rather a special function relegated to a certain caste. It is now something performed for them. It is no longer religious worship, but a religious performance. The pulpit has become a stage on which polished actors present a dramatic performance for a stipulated fee.

The decay of Protestantism is not due to abandonment of the priestly office, but to the fact that a watered down version of it is still maintained. When the Romish priest speaks about "churches ceasing to be temples" he uses both words in a sense that no inspired apostle ever employed when talking about the kingdom of heaven. The word "church" was never applied to a material structure in the Sacred Scriptures; nor did God ever in the New Covenant sanction "a temple" made of wood and stone. The "house of God" is made up of living stones. The children of God do not go to God's house—they are God's house! We are "built upon the foundation of the apostles and prophets, Christ Jesus himself being the chief cornerstone, in whom the whole structure is joined together and grows into a holy temple in the Lord."

The priesthood of the Roman Catholic Church is not a divinely established agency. It can satisfy no real spiritual hunger, although it may serve to allay the fears of superstitious ignorance. It does not provide the bread of life, but stands between the hungry soul and Him who has that bread. It obscures the true meaning of God's altar and sacrifice, His priesthood and worship. The priestcraft of Rome is a burlesque upon God's holy provision, a deliberate attempt upon the part of sinful man to rob God's family of their paternal rights. It is destitute of divine authority, an arrogant usurper, and an unholy claimant of divine rights. May God deliver the people from this blight!

A SINCERE APPEAL

When Ezekiel was carried a captive into Babylon, the city of Jerusalem was not yet destroyed. One day the prophet was sitting in his foreign house with some of the elders of Judah, when he saw a dazzling vision. A man appeared who took him by a lock of his hair, and the Spirit lifted him up between heaven and earth, and transported him in a trance to Jerusalem. There he was forced to look upon the idolatrous practices carried out in secret and also openly on the very porch of the temple (Ezek. 8). The city was almost wholly filled with worshippers of pagan deities.

As the prophet contemplated the wretched scene, he saw seven men approaching from the direction of the upper gate. Six of these held drawn swords, the seventh had a writing case at his side. They marched solemnly into the temple precincts and stood beside the bronze altar. A voice called out instructions to the man with the writing case, "Go through the city, through Jerusalem, and put a mark upon the foreheads of the men who sigh and groan over all the abominations that are committed in it." The other six were then ordered to pass through the city behind the first, and to slay outright, without pity, all who were not marked in their foreheads. They were told positively to "touch no one upon whom is the mark." And they were likewise told to "begin at my sanctuary."

We believe that idolatry, worldliness and apostasy characterize much of the religious world in these days. The leaders are like the false prophets in the time of Ezekiel. "They have spoken falsehood and divined a lie, they say, 'Says the Lord,' when the Lord has not sent them, and yet they expect him to fulfill their word. Have you not seen a delusive vision, and uttered a lying divination, whenever you have said 'Says the Lord,' although I have not spoken?" (Ezek. 13: 6, 7). Yet there must be in this Babylon of religion, hundreds of honest and humble hearts who sigh and groan over the abominations committed in the name of worship. Surely the invisible mark on the forehead has been made by the one whose finger wrote on the temple walls of Belshazzar. "The Lord knoweth them that are his." The judgment of God will be upon this idolatrous generation. That judgment will begin in his sanctuary.

The sectarian spirit of today can never achieve the ideal of God. It can never answer the prayer for unity of Him "whom having not seen we love." Division, schism and strife are perpetuated by the clergy. The common people sigh for unity. They do not want to hate their fellowmen, but they are taught prejudice, animosity and fear by leaders who segregate them with human creeds as barriers to prevent them from thinking for themselves. The early Christians belonged to no sect. They had no other creed but Christ. They were not fractured into divers groups, each with a top echelon of clergymen who exploited them for gain and manipulated them for political prestige. They were all a kingdom of priests unto God, and they recognized no high priest but the Son of God, now coronated King of kings.

Greed for money is at the bottom of much of our sad plight. Men make a profession of dispensing the water of life which God has freely given to all. They then inaugurate a special caste to minister in this profession and demand support from the rest of God's children. Others see an opportunity to make gain and seize power by instituting organizations to produce and train the professional clergymen. Theological seminaries operating as specialized colleges are begun and again a tax is levied against the "clergy of God" to produce a special clergy which will steal the very privileges of those who pay tribute to this earthly handmaiden to produce them. Eventually the simplicity of God's original plan of priesthood becomes so obscure, that those who plead for a return to the old paths are derided, maligned and laughed to scorn.

Occasionally, men who love the cause of Christ and sigh for its purity rise up and sound the call to return to Jerusalem. The hearts of men are stirred for a brief time, and the weary marchers take up their burdens and face again toward the walls of Zion. But the love of popularity, the lust for pre-eminence, the desire for gain soon crush out the noble ambition, and once again a clever priestcraft under innocent titles takes over and the work bogs down in a morass of innovations.

L. F. Bittle, writing in *Apostolic Messenger,* September, 1918, said: "And when we look at the various reformations that have been started, we see that they all follow the same general course. Beginning with an enthusiastic love of truth and a willingness to sacrifice even life on its behalf, they soon degenerate into formalism and selfishness. The reformers left their creeds to bind the minds of their successors, but they could not leave their spirits to stir their hearts. Rescued from priestcraft, their followers soon made a priesthood of their own to repeat in another form the follies and frauds of the past.

"What has been called the Current Reformation is rapidly sharing the fate of its predecessors. The scriptural knowledge, the zeal for the primitive faith and order, the love and unity in the truth that characterized the earlier stages of the work, are passing away, and the desire to be like the sects around them is transforming the Reformers into a priest-led people who are hurrying down toward Babylon as eagerly as they once struggled up to Jerusalem. Such is the result of exchanging principle for policy and of adopting the suggestions of human wisdom instead of adhering strictly to the oracles of God. And the folly and wickedness of the procedure appear the greater when we remember the Reformers had the mistakes of their predecessors to warn them of the danger of going beyond the things that are written."

If this generation is to see any rapid strides toward restoration of the New Testament order it must begin with the elimination of the whole clergy idea, under whatsoever name or system that idea is perpetuated. Labeling poison by a harmless name does not change its nature, but makes it the more dangerous. There must be a purging from our very thinking of a clergy system which is repugnant to God. The humble and saintly David King said in a paper which he read at the annual meeting of the churches of Christ, in Leeds (England) in 1876: "Nothing seems more opposed to the genius of the Christian system than the recognition of a class of professionals paid for preaching, as are lawyers for pleading, and doctors for prescribing, irrespective of need." In the same speech he also declared: "Paying one man to fill the pulpit with a view to keep up preaching and worship acceptable to a stated congregation, whether that man be called evangelist or pastor, almost invariably exiles New Testament order." Again he remarks: "I have done so much preaching and am therefore entitled to so much pay whether needed or otherwise is both illogical and a burlesque of Christian propagandism."

But how shall we rid ourselves of the burden of an unscriptural clergy system? That the task will be difficult let no one doubt. The first step must be a firm resolution to examine the sacred Scriptures by each child of God for himself. Everyone who loves God must not only seek to derive spiritual food for his own growth, but he must have then a compelling urge to share his learning with his brethren for their good. Restoration must always be preceded by reformation —of life, thinking, attitude and heart. Let the glorious liberty which is ours in Christ Jesus be again understood and cherished. Let anything which will steal that liberty and bring us again into bondage be so obnoxious to us that we will not countenance even the faintest hint of it.

Men must reassert their right to "buy wine and milk without money and without price" (Isa. 55: 1). They must resent with every moral fiber the idea of professionals "cashing in on the gospel" and selling back to them that which God gave equally to all mankind. They must be possessed of such an over-powering love for undying souls that they will all carry the glad tidings to loved ones, friends and neighbors. They must be willing to share in the problem of edifying the congregation both privately and "when the whole congregation is come together in one place."

It is not a question with real saints whether a thing will work or not. The only thing they question is whether or not it is God's will. If it is they must make it work. God's plan will work if we will work God's plan.

Many preachers are unwilling victims of a modern condition which they secretly detest and even openly question. They realize that the position which they occupy as "The Minister" in a local congregation is without scriptural warrant. Such men must through prayer and meditation strengthen their hearts and steel their convictions until they develop the courage to break away from tradition and cease to cater to that which will enslave the Church. This will require a tremendous faith, because of the adverse criticism, and the tug of so many considerations which may be sacrificed—money, power and prestige!

The wives of such gospel preachers will need to be saintly women. The feminine heart seeks security. There is a lure in a nice home made ready to the hands, in a regular check of ample proportions, in the social glory attending a profession. To turn one's back upon all such appeals and face the future is an acid test of fidelity to God. Yet in every age there have not been wanting faithful women who have encouraged their men to "stand fast in the Lord."

All must be made to realize that the task of bringing the world to Christ belongs to every saint. The realization of that fact overturned paganism in the first few centuries after Christ. It is the only thing which can do it again. "It is an interesting, but not a surprising fact, that the circumstances of the first planting of Christianity in places which later were among its most powerful seats, including Rome and Carthage, are not known. Visitors to Jerusalem at the great festivals, mechanics who changed their abode from place to place, and commercial travellers, might carry to their homes the faith which they had elsewhere received and form the nucleus of Christian communities. The gospel doctrine was transported from place to place, as seeds are blown from the trees and wafted abroad" (*The Beginning of Christianity*—Fisher).

The first truly literary assailant of Christianity was Celsus, who about the beginning of the second century taunted God's congregation with the fact that "wool-workers, cobblers, leather-dressers, the most illiterate and vulgar of mankind, were zealous preachers of the gospel."

One historian declares: "If men were often, in the first instance, won without the word, they were won to the word, and to Him who gave it. And the word was nigh unto them. It dropped from the lips of those whose lives adorned it, and it is a most notable circumstance that, though there was a regular ministry from the beginning, there is scarcely anything said in the history of the second and third centuries of Christians who could, in any distinctive sense, be called missionaries. The trader on his journey, the soldier in the camp, the slave in the house, the philosopher among his disciples, as well as the friend among friends and the mother among her children: these all did their part in diffusing the knowledge of the truth which they felt to be of God, and to which, they were assured, God would give the victory" (*The Early Church*, by David Duff, M.A., D.D., LL.D.)

In the primitive church the saints met to worship and scattered to preach. The bench of the cobbler, the plowhandles of the farmer, the desk of the tax collector; these were the only pulpits known. The Christians took the good news to the world; they did not build houses and tell the world to come. The kingdom was spread like leaven works in the dough. Just as the yeast affects one particle of the mixture and it then permeates every other particle with which it comes in contact, so Christianity filled the hearts of men, and from them spread to other hearts as they came in contact in the pursuit of daily tasks. The slave girl whispered the story of freedom into the ear of her haughty mistress as she combed her tresses and applied the unguent; the bazaar keeper talked to the prospective purchasers as they examined his wares; the banker heard about the lowly Nazarene at the public bath; the clerk in his counting house; the farmer at the local inn. The Ethiopian treasurer learned of Christ as he rode along in his chariot; the jailer in his dungeon keep; Lydia out on the river bank. Everywhere men were persuaded by those who said, "We have found him of whom the prophets have spoken."

Those who were Christians did not speak of "entering the ministry." They were already in it. Everyone entered the ministry at baptism. To be in Christ was to be in the ministry. No one went away to study for "the Ministry." Each one began where he was and announced the Messiah who had come. People did not send for a preacher. They just began preaching. All who had been inducted into the kingdom could tell what they did and why they did it. Every Christian was a minister, everyone was a priest. The congregation was a priesthood—a royal priesthood composed of all believers.

Each week these priests gathered about a table. They ate of the bread and drank of the cup in memory of the Lord's death. As they were assembled they prayed. Their prayers were spontaneous. They did not pray because they were "on the program" or because they were "assigned to do it." They talked to God as a son speaks with his father. They bore their mutual burdens to the throne to find grace to help in time of need. They rejoiced in thanksgiving in the presence of God. They spoke to each other to build up, stir up and cheer up.

Their talks were not formal or stilted sermons. A number of brethren participated, speaking one by one, that all might be edified and all might be comforted.

The pattern of religious worship in the early church was designed by God to meet the needs of the church in all ages. It requires no alteration, needs no amendment, and demands no improvement. The church of today can only be healthy if it follows this prototype. To produce it we must first alter our views concerning the word "member." We employ it today to designate one who has united with a specific congregation, or who has his name on the roster of the local church. We talk about "a member of the church" in the same sense that we refer to a member of the country club, a lodge or a farm bureau. The word is never so employed in the New Testament. There it always refers to one who sustains a vital, living connection with the spiritual body of our Lord, and who is thus in direct relation to Him as the head. And just as one does not confer about the problem of finding something for his physical hands, ears or feet, to do, so we should not have to discuss putting the members of Christ to work.

When a child, is born, we never once question how many of his physical members will be, or should be, employed in the growth of his body. We train him in the use of his members as he grows toward maturity, but if someone were to advance the idea that a majority of the members should be bound and not permitted to function lest they embarrass the rest of the members, such a person would be laughed out of court. It is only in the spiritual body that we devise schemes whereby the majority of the members can shift their responsibility to one hired to do the work. Such a system not only degrades God's spiritual institution, making of it a helpless, dependent and servile thing, but worst of all, it appropriates the privileges and abrogates the rights of those who are truly priests of God.

The call to a brighter and better day goes forth to all who are of a broken and contrite spirit. The way to liberty in Christ Jesus is the way of the cross. Men who plead for a complete restoration of the New Testament church must endure persecution and misrepresentation. An organization in its corruption never did, and never will, admit it. Its only feeling will be anger, not repentance. There is no hope of reforming a decadent movement as a body. The only hope is that men will arise who see the need to call forth those whose trust is stayed in God and once more start a move toward Jerusalem's broken down walls.

Our plea is to everyone who has a good and honest heart. Only on such fertile soil will the seed of the kingdom produce a bountiful yield. Regardless of religious affiliation in the past, of parental instruction, ecclesiastical tradition, or priestly doctrine, let us throw off the yoke which neither we nor our fathers were able to bear. Let us recapture the fountain of life so that its waters can once more flow *free* and *freely*, and restore to this earth the congregation as it was given by Him who is our great high priest at the right hand of God. Remember that "you also as living stones are built up a spiritual house, a holy priesthood, to offer up spiritual sacrifices acceptable to God by Jesus Christ." May God bless the royal priesthood of all believers is our very humble and sincere prayer.